NUMBER PROPERTIES

GRE Math Strategy Guide

The Number Properties guide provides a comprehensive analysis of the properties and rules of integers tested on the GRE, addressing topics from prime products to consecutive integers.

D1315982

Number Properties GRE Strategy Guide, Second Edition

10-digit International Standard Book Number: 1-935707-50-7
13-digit International Standard Book Number: 978-1-935707-50-9
eISBN: 978-0-984178-02-5

8 GUIDE INSTRUCTIONAL SERIES

Math GRE Preparation Guides

Algebra
(ISBN: 978-1-935707-47-9)

Fractions, Decimals, & Percents
(ISBN: 978-1-935707-48-6)

Geometry
(ISBN: 978-1-935707-49-3)

Number Properties
(ISBN: 978-1-935707-50-9)

Word Problems
(ISBN: 978-1-935707-54-7)

Quantitative Comparisons & Data Interpretation
(ISBN: 978-1-935707-51-6)

Verbal GRE Preparation Guides

Reading Comprehension & Essays
(ISBN: 978-1-935707-52-3)

Text Completion & Sentence Equivalence
(ISBN: 978-1-935707-53-0)

Manhattan GRE

March 15th, 2011

Dear Student,

Thank you for picking up one of the Manhattan GRE Strategy Guides—we hope that it ends up being just what you need to prepare for the new GRE.

As with most accomplishments, there were many people involved in the book that you're holding. First and foremost is Zeke Vanderhoek, the founder of MG Prep. Zeke was a lone tutor in New York when he started the Company in 2000. Now, eleven years later, the Company has Instructors and offices nationwide and contributes to the studies and successes of thousands of students each year.

Our Manhattan GRE Strategy Guides are based on the continuing experiences of our Instructors and our students. On the Company side, we are indebted to many of our Instructors, including but not limited to Roman Altshuler, Chris Berman, Faruk Bursal, Jen Dziura, Dmitry Farber, Stacey Koprince, David Mahler, Seb Moosapoor, Stephanie Moyerman, Chris Ryan, Michael Schwartz, Tate Shafer, Emily Sledge, Tommy Wallach, and Ryan Wessel, all of whom either wrote or edited the books to their present form. Dan McNaney and Cathy Huang provided their formatting expertise to make the books as user-friendly as possible. Last, many people, too numerous to list here but no less appreciated, assisted in the development of the online resources that accompany this guide.

At Manhattan GRE, we continually aspire to provide the best Instructors and resources possible. We hope that you'll find our dedication manifest in this book. If you have any comments or questions, please e-mail me at dan@manhattangre.com. I'll be sure that your comments reach our curriculum team—and I'll read them too.

Best of luck in preparing for the GRE!

Sincerely,

Dan

Dan Gonzalez
Managing Director
Manhattan GRE

HOW TO ACCESS YOUR ONLINE STUDENT CENTER

If you...

⊙ **are a registered Manhattan GRE student**

and have received this book as part of your course materials, you have AUTOMATIC access to ALL of our online resources. To access these resources, follow the instructions in the Welcome Guide provided to you at the start of your program. Do NOT follow the instructions below.

⊙ **purchased this book from the Manhattan GRE Online store or at one of our Centers**

1. Go to: http://www.manhattangre.com/studentcenter.cfm

2. Log in using the username and password used when your account was set up. Your one year of online access begins on the day that you purchase the book from the Manhattan GRE online store or at one of our centers.

⊙ **purchased this book at a retail location**

1. Go to: http://www.manhattangre.com/access.cfm

2. Log in or create an account.

3. Follow the instructions on the screen.

Your one year of online access begins on the day that you register your book at the above URL.

You only need to register your product ONCE at the above URL. To use your online resources any time AFTER you have completed the registration process, login to the following URL: http://www.manhattangre.com/studentcenter.cfm

Please note that online access is non-transferable. This means that only NEW and UNREGISTERED copies of the book will grant you online access. Previously used books will not provide any online resources.

⊙ **purchased an e-book version of this book**

1. Create an account with Manhattan GRE at the website: https://www.manhattangre.com/createaccount.cfm

2. Email a copy of your purchase receipt to books@manhattangre.com to activate your resources. Please be sure to use the same email address to create an account that you used to purchase the e-book.

For any technical issues, email books@manhattangre.com or call 646-254-6479.

TABLE OF CONTENTS

g

Chapter 1
of
NUMBER PROPERTIES

INTRODUCTION &
THE REVISED GRE

In This Chapter . . .

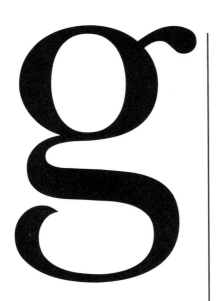

- Introduction, and How to Use Manhattan GRE's Strategy Guides

- The Revised GRE

- Question Formats in Detail

Introduction, and How to Use Manhattan GRE's Strategy Guides

We know that you're looking to succeed on the GRE so that you can go to graduate school and do the things you want to do in life.

We also know that you might not have done math since high school, and that you may never have learned words like "adumbrate" or "sangfroid." We know that it's going to take hard work on your part to get a top GRE score, and that's why we've put together the only set of books that will take you from the basics all the way up to the material you need to master for a near-perfect score, or whatever your score goal may be. You've taken the first step. Now it's time to get to work!

How to Use These Materials

Manhattan GRE's materials are comprehensive. But keep in mind that, depending on your score goal, it may not be necessary to "get" absolutely everything. Grad schools only see your overall Quantitative, Verbal, and Writing scores—they don't see exactly which strengths and weaknesses went into creating those scores.

You may be enrolled in one of our courses, in which case you already have a syllabus telling you in what order you should approach the books. But if you bought this book online or at a bookstore, feel free to approach the books—and even the chapters within the books—in whatever order works best for you. *For the most part, the books, and the chapters within them, are independent; you don't have to master one section before moving on to the next.* So if you're having a hard time with something in particular, you can make a note to come back to it later and move on to another section. Similarly, it may not be necessary to solve every single practice problem for every section. As you go through the material, continually assess whether you understand and can apply the principles in each individual section and chapter. The best way to do this is to solve the Check Your Skills and Practice Problems throughout. If you're confident you have a concept or method down, feel free to move on. If you struggle with something, make note of it for further review. Stay active in your learning and oriented toward the test—it's easy to read something and think you understand it, only to have trouble applying it in the 1–2 minutes you have to solve a problem.

Study Skills

As you're studying for the GRE, try to integrate your learning into your everyday life. For example, vocabulary is a big part of the GRE, as well as something you just can't "cram" for—you're going to want to do at least a little bit of vocab every day. So, try to learn and internalize a little bit at a time, switching up topics often to help keep things interesting.

Keep in mind that, while many of your study materials are on paper (including ETS's most recent source of official GRE questions, *The Official Guide to the GRE revised General Test*), your exam will be administered on a computer. Because this is a computer-based test, you will NOT be able to underline portions of reading passages, write on diagrams of geometry figures, or otherwise physically mark up problems. So get used to this now. Solve the problems in these books on scratch paper. (Each of our books talks specifically about what to write down for different problem types).

Again, as you study stay focused on the test-day experience. As you progress, work on timed drills and sets of questions. Eventually, you should be taking full practice tests (available at www.manhattangre.com) under actual timed conditions.

The Revised GRE

As of August 1, 2011, the Quantitative and Verbal sections of the GRE will undergo a number of changes. The actual body of knowledge being tested won't change, but the *way* it is tested will. Here's a brief summary of what to expect, followed by a more comprehensive assessment of the new exam.

Overall, the general format of the test will change. The length of the test will increase from about 3.5 hours to about 4 hours. There will be two scored math sections and two scored verbal sections rather than one of each, and a new score scale of 130–170 will be used in place of the old 200–800 scale. More on this later.

The Verbal section of the GRE will change dramatically. The Analogies and Antonym questions will disappear. The Sentence Completions and Reading Comprehension will remain, to be expanded and remixed in a few new ways. Vocabulary will still be important, but only in the context of complete sentences. That is, you'll no longer have to worry about vocabulary words standing alone. So for those who dislike learning vocabulary words, the changes will provide partial relief. For those who were looking forward to getting lots of points just for memorizing words, the Manhattan GRE verbal strategy guides will prepare you for the shift.

The Quant section of the GRE prior to August 1, 2011 is composed of multiple choice problems, Quantitative Comparisons, and Data Interpretation questions (which are really a subset of multiple choice problems). The revised test will contain two new problem formats in addition to the current problem formats. However, the type of math, and the difficulty of the math, will remain unchanged.

Additionally, a small four-function calculator with a square root button will appear on-screen. Many test takers will rejoice at the advent of this calculator! It is true that the GRE calculator will reduce emphasis on computation—but look out for problems, such as percents questions with tricky wording, that are likely to foil those who rely on the calculator too much. *In short, the calculator may make your life a bit easier from time to time, but you will never <u>need</u> the calculator to solve a problem.*

Finally, don't worry about whether these new problem types are "harder" or "easier." You are being judged against other test takers, all of whom are in the same boat. So if the new formats are harder, they are harder for other test takers as well.

Exam Structure

The revised test has six sections. You will get a ten-minute break between the third and fourth sections and a one-minute break between the others. The Analytical Writing section is always first. The other five sections can be seen in any order and will include:

- Two Verbal Reasoning sections (approximately 20 questions each in exactly 30 minutes per section)

- Two Quantitative Reasoning sections (approximately 20 questions each in exactly 35 minutes per section)

- Either an "unscored" section or a "research" section

An unscored section will look just like a third Verbal or Quantitative Reasoning section, and you will not be told which of them doesn't count. If you get a research section, it will be identified as such.

Section Type	# Questions	Time	Scored?
Analytical Writing	2 essays	30 minutes each	Yes
Verbal #1	Approx. 20	30 minutes	Yes
Quantitative #1	Approx. 20	35 minutes	Yes
Verbal #2	Approx. 20	30 minutes	Yes
Quantitative #2	Approx. 20	35 minutes	Yes
Unscored Section (verbal or quant)	Approx. 20	30 or 35 min	No
Research Section	Varies	Varies	No

10 min break

one or the other, but not both

order varies

Later in the chapter, we'll look at all the question formats in detail.

Using the Calculator

The addition of a small, four-function calculator with a square root button means that those taking the revised test can forget re-memorizing their times tables or square roots. However, the calculator is not a cure-all; in many problems, the difficulty is in figuring out what numbers to put into the calculator in the first place. In some cases, using a calculator will actually be less helpful than doing the problem some other way. Let's look at an example:

> If x is the remainder when (11)(7) is divided by 4 and y is the remainder when (14)(6) is divided by 13, what is the value of $x + y$?

Solution: This problem is designed so that the calculator won't tell the whole story. Certainly the calculator will tell us that $11 \times 7 = 77$. When you divide 77 by 4, however, the calculator yields an answer of 19.25. The remainder is *not* 0.25 (a remainder is always a whole number).

You might just go back to your pencil and paper, and find the largest multiple of 4 that is less than 77. Since 4 DOES go into 76, we can conclude that 4 would leave a remainder of 1 when dividing into 77. (Notice that we don't even need to know how many times 4 goes into 76, just that it goes in. One way to mentally "jump" to 76 is to say, *4 goes into 40, so it goes into 80 … that's a bit too big, so take away 4 to get 76.*) You could also multiply the leftover 0.25 times 4 (the divisor) to find the remainder of 1.

However, it is also possible to use the calculator to find a remainder. Divide 77 by 4 to get 19.25. Thus, 4 goes into 77 nineteen times, with a remainder left over. Now use your calculator to multiply 19 (JUST 19, not 19.25) by 4. You will get 76. The remainder is $77 - 76 = 1$. Therefore, $x = 1$.

Use the same technique to find y. Multiply 14×6 to get 84. Divide 84 by 13 to get 6.46… Ignore everything after the decimal, and just multiply 6 by 13 to get 78. The remainder is therefore $84 - 78 = 6$. Therefore, $y = 6$.

Since we are looking for $x + y$ and $1 + 6 = 7$, the answer is 7.

You can see that blind faith in the calculator can be dangerous. Use it responsibly! And this leads us to…

Practice Using the Calculator!

On the new GRE, the on-screen calculator will slow you down or lead to incorrect answers if you're not careful! If you plan to use the thing on test day (which you should), you'll want to pactice first.

We have created an online practice calculator for your use. To access this calculator, go to www.manhattangre.com and sign in to the student center using the instructions on the "How to Access Your Online Student Center" page found at the front of this book.

In addition to the calculator, you will see instructions for how to use the calculator. Be sure to read these instructions and work through the associated exercises. Throughout our math books, you will see the symbol. This symbol means "use the calculator here!" As much as possible, have the online practice calculator up and running during your review of our math books. You'll have the chance to use the on-screen calculator when you take our practice exams as well.

Navigating the Questions in a Section

Another change for test takers on the new GRE is the ability to move freely around the questions in a section… you can go forward and backward one-by-one and can even jump directly to any question from the "review list." The review list provides a snapshot of which questions you have answered, which ones you have tagged for "mark and review," and which are incomplete, either because you didn't select enough answers or because you selected too many (that is, if a number of choices is specified by the question). You should double-check the review list for completion if you finish the section early. Using the review list feature will take some practice as well, which is why we've built it into our online practice exams. Here's some introductory advice.

The majority of test takers will be pressed for time. Thus, for most of you, it won't be feasible to "go back to" multiple problems at the end of the section. Generally, if you can't get a question the first time, you won't be able to get it the second time around either. With this in mind, here's how we recommend using the new review list feature.

1. Do the questions in order as they appear.

2. When you encounter a difficult question, do you best to eliminate answer choices you know are wrong.

3. If you're not sure of an answer, take an educated guess from the choices remaining. Do <u>NOT</u> skip it and hope to return to it later.

4. Using the "mark" button at the top of the screen, mark up to three questions per section that you think you might be able to solve with more time. Mark a question only after you have taken an educated guess.

5. If you have time at the end of the section, click on the review list, identify any questions you've marked and return to them. If you do not have any time remaining, you will have already taken good guesses at the tough ones.

What you want to avoid is "surfing"—clicking forward and backward through the questions searching for the easy ones. This will eat up valuable time. Of course, you'll want to move through the tough ones quickly if you can't get them, but try to avoid skipping stuff.

Again, all of this will take practice. Use our practice exams to fine-tune your approach.

Scoring

Two things have changed about the scoring of the Verbal Reasoning and Quantitative Reasoning sections: (1) how individual questions influence the score and (2) the score scale itself.

For both the Verbal Reasoning and Quantitative Reasoning sections, you will receive a raw score, which is simply how many questions you answered correctly. Your raw score is converted to a scaled score, accounting for the difficulties of the specific questions you actually saw.

The old GRE was question-adaptive, meaning that your answer to each question (right or wrong) determined, at least somewhat, the questions that followed (harder or easier). Because you had to commit to an answer to let the algorithm do its thing, you weren't allowed to skip questions or go back to change answers. On the revised GRE, the adapting will occur from section to section (e.g., if you do well on the first verbal section, you will get a harder second verbal section) rather than from question to question. The only change test takers will notice is one most will welcome: you can now move freely about the questions in a section, coming back to tough questions later, changing answers after "ah-ha!" moments, and generally managing your time more flexibly.

The scores for the revised GRE Quantitative Reasoning and Verbal Reasoning will be reported on a 130 to 170 scale in 1-point increments, whereas the old score reporting was on a 200 to 800 scale in 10-point increments. You will receive one 130–170 score for verbal and a separate 130–170 score for quant. If you are already putting your GRE math skills to work, you may notice that there are now 41 scores possible (170 – 130, then add one before you're done), whereas before there were 61 scores possible ([800 – 200]/10, then add one before you're done). In other words, a 10 point difference on the old score scale actually indicated a smaller performance differential than a 1 point difference on the new scale. However, the GRE folks argue that perception is reality: the difference between 520 and 530 on the old scale could simply seem greater than the difference between 151 and 152 on the new scale. If that's true, then this change will benefit test-takers, who won't be unfairly compared by schools for minor differences in performance. If not true, then the change will be moot.

Important Dates

Registration for the GRE revised General Test opens on March 15, 2011, and the first day of testing with the new format is August 1, 2011.

Perhaps to encourage people to take the revised exam, rather than rushing to take the old exam before the change or waiting "to see what happens" with the new exam long after August 1, 2011, ETS is offering a 50% discount on the test fee for anyone who takes the revised test from August 1 through September 30, 2011. Scores for people who take the revised exam in this discount period will be sent starting in mid- to late-November. This implies that you may have to wait up to 3.5 months to get your score during this rollout period!

By December 2011, ETS expects to resume normal score reporting schedules: score reports will be sent a mere 10-15 days after the test date.

IMPORTANT: If you need GRE scores before mid-November 2011 to meet a school deadline, take the "old" GRE no later than July 31, 2011! Waiting to take the revised test not only would require you to study for a different test, but also would delay your score reporting.

Question Formats in Detail

Essay Questions

The Analytical Writing section consists of two separately timed 30-minute tasks: Analyze an Issue and Analyze an Argument. As you can imagine, the 30-minute time limit implies that you aren't aiming to write an essay that would garner a Pulitzer Prize nomination, but rather to complete the tasks adequately and according to the directions. Each essay is scored separately, but your reported essay score is the average of the two rounded up to the next half-point increment on a 0 to 6 scale.

Issue Task—This essay prompt will present a claim, generally one that is vague enough to be interpreted in various ways and discussed from numerous perspectives. Your job as a test taker is to write a response discussing the extent to which you agree or disagree and support your position. Don't sit on the fence—pick a side!

For some examples of Issue Task prompts, visit the GRE website here:

http://www.ets.org/gre/revised_general/prepare/analytical_writing/issue/pool

Argument Task—This essay prompt will be an argument comprised of both a claim(s) and evidence. Your job is to dispassionately discuss the argument's structural flaws and merits (well, mostly the flaws). Don't agree or disagree with the argument—evaluate its logic.

For some examples of Argument Task prompts, visit the GRE website here:

http://www.ets.org/gre/revised_general/prepare/analytical_writing/argument/pool

Verbal: Reading Comprehension Questions

Standard 5-choice multiple choice reading comprehension questions will continue to appear on the new exam. You are likely familiar with how these work. Let's take a look at two *new* reading comprehension formats that will appear on the new test.

Select One or More Answer Choices and Select-in-Passage

For the question type, "Select One or More Answer Choices," you are given three statements about a passage and asked to "select all that apply." Either one, two, or all three can be correct (there is no "none of the above" option). There is no partial credit; you must select all the correct choices and none of the incorrect choices.

Strategy Tip: On "Select One or More Answer Choices," don't let your brain be tricked into telling you "Well, if two of them have been right so far, the other one must be wrong," or any other arbitrary idea about how many of the choices "should" be correct. Make sure to consider each choice independently! You cannot use "Process of Elimination" the same way as you do on "normal" multiple-choice questions.

For the question type "Select-in-Passage," you are given an assignment such as "Select the sentence in the passage that explains why the experiment's results were discovered to be invalid." Clicking anywhere on the sentence in the passage will highlight it. (As with any GRE question, you will have to click "Confirm" to submit your answer, so don't worry about accidentally selecting the wrong sentence due to a slip of the mouse.)

Strategy Tip: On "Select-in-Passage," if the passage is short, consider numbering each sentence (that is, writing 1 2 3 4 on your paper) and crossing off each choice as you determine that it isn't the answer. If the passage is long, you might write a number for each paragraph (I, II, III), and tick off each number as you determine that the correct sentence is not located in that paragraph.

Now let's give these new question types a try!

The sample questions below are based on this passage:

> Physicist Robert Oppenheimer, director of the fateful Manhattan Project, said "It is a profound and necessary truth that the deep things in science are not found because they are useful; they are found because it was possible to find them." In a later address at MIT, Oppenheimer presented the thesis that scientists could be held only very nominally responsible for the consequences of their research and discovery. Oppenheimer asserted that ethics, philosophy, and politics have very little to do with the day-to-day work of the scientist, and that scientists could not rationally be expected to predict all the effects of their work. Yet, in a talk in 1945 to the Association of Los Alamos Scientists, Oppenheimer offered some reasons why the Manhattan project scientists built the atomic bomb; the justifications included "fear that Nazi Germany would build it first" and "hope that it would shorten the war."

For question #1, consider each of the three choices separately and select all that apply.

1. The passage implies that Robert Oppenheimer would most likely have agreed with which of the following views:

   A Some scientists take military goals into account in their work
   B Deep things in science are not useful
   C The everyday work of a scientist is only minimally involved with ethics

2. Select the sentence in which the writer implies that Oppenheimer has not been consistent in his view that scientists have little consideration for the effects of their work.

[Here, you would highlight the appropriate sentence with your mouse. Note that there are only four options.]

Solutions:

1. {A, C} Oppenheimer says in the last sentence that one of the reasons the bomb was built was scientists' "hope that it would shorten the war." Thus, Oppenheimer would likely agree with the view that "Some scientists take military goals into account in their work." B is a trap answer using familiar language from the passage. Oppenheimer says that scientific discoveries' possible usefulness is not why scientists make discoveries; he does not say that the discoveries aren't useful. Oppenheimer specifically says that ethics has "very little to do with the day-to-day work of the scientist," which is a good match for "only minimally involved with ethics."

   Strategy Tip: On "Select One or More Answer Choices," write ABC on your paper and mark each choice with a check, an X, or a symbol such as ~ if you're not sure. This should keep you from crossing out all three choices and having to go back (at least one of the choices must be correct). For example, let's say that on a different question you had marked

       A. X
       B. X
       C. ~

   The one you weren't sure about, (C), is likely to be correct, since there must be at least one correct answer.

2. The correct sentence is: **Yet, in a talk in 1945 to the Association of Los Alamos Scientists, Oppenheimer offered some reasons why the Manhattan project scientists built the atomic bomb; the justifications included "fear that Nazi Germany would build it first" and "hope that it would shorten the war."** The word "yet" is a good clue that this sentence is about to express a view contrary to the views expressed in the rest of the passage.

Verbal: Text Completion Questions

Text Completions are the new, souped-up Sentence Completions. They can consist of 1–5 sentences with 1–3 blanks. When Text Completions have two or three blanks, you will select words for those blanks independently. There is no partial credit; you must make every selection correctly.

Because this makes things a bit harder, the GRE has kindly reduced the number of possible choices per blank from five to three. Here is an old two-blank Sentence Completion, as it would appear on the old GRE:

Old Format:

> Leaders are not always expected to _____ the same rules as are those they lead; leaders are often looked up to for a surety and presumption that would be viewed as _____ in most others.
>
>   A. obey … avarice
>
>   B. proscribe … insalubriousness
>
>   C. decree … anachronism
>
>   D. conform to … hubris
>
>   E. follow … eminence

And here's how this same sentence would appear on the new exam.

New Format:

> Leaders are not always expected to (i) _____ the same rules as are those they lead; leaders are often looked up to for a surety and presumption that would be viewed as (ii) _____ in most others.

Blank (i)		Blank (ii)
decree		hubris
proscribe		avarice
conform to		anachronism

On the new GRE, you will select your two choices by actually clicking and highlighting the words you want.

Solution:

In the first blank, we need a word similar to "follow." In the second blank, we need a word similar to "arrogant." Only choice D works in the old format; in the new format, the answer is still "conform to" and "hubris," but you'll make the two choices separately.

Note that in the "Old Format" question, if you knew that you needed a word in the second blank that meant something like "arrogant," and you knew that "hubris" was the only word in the second column with the correct meaning, you could pick correct answer choice D without even considering the first word in each pair. In the new format, this strategy is no longer available to us.

Also note that, in the "Old Format" question, "obey," "conform to," and "follow" mean basically the same thing. On the new GRE, this can't happen: since you select each word independently, no two choices can be synonyms (otherwise, there would be two correct answers).

Strategy Tip: As on the old GRE, do NOT look at the answer choices until you've decided for yourself, based on textual clues actually written in the sentence, what kind of word needs to go in each blank. Only then should you look at the choices and eliminate those that are not matches.

Let's try an example with three blanks.

> For Kant, the fact of having a right and having the (i) _____ to enforce it via coercion cannot be separated, and he asserts that this marriage of rights and coercion is compatible with the freedom of everyone. This is not at all peculiar from the standpoint of modern political thought—what good is a right if its violation triggers no enforcement (be it punishment or (ii) _____)? The necessity of coercion is not at all in conflict with the freedom of everyone, because this coercion only comes into play when someone has (iii)_____ someone else.

Blank (ii)	Blank (ii)	Blank (iii)
technique	amortization	questioned the hypothesis of
license	reward	violated the rights of
prohibition	restitution	granted civil liberties to

Solution:

In the first sentence, use the clue "he asserts that this marriage of rights and coercion is compatible with the freedom of everyone" to help fill in the first blank. Kant believes that "coercion" is "married to" rights and is compatible with freedom for all. So we want something in the first blank like "right" or "power." Kant believes that rights are meaningless without enforcement. Only the choice "license" can work (while a "license" can be physical, like a driver's license, "license" can also mean "right").

The second blank is part of the phrase "punishment or _____," which we are told is the "enforcement" resulting from the violation of a right. So the blank should be something, other than punishment, that constitutes enforcement against someone who violates a right. (More simply, it should be something bad!) Only "restitution" works. Restitution is compensating the victim in some way (perhaps monetarily or by returning stolen goods).

In the final sentence, "coercion only comes into play when someone has _____ someone else." Throughout the text, "coercion" means enforcement against someone who has violated the rights of someone else. The meaning is the same here. The answer is "violated the rights of."

The complete and correct answer is this combination:

Blank (i)	Blank (ii)	Blank (iii)
license	restitution	violated the rights of

In theory, there are $3 \times 3 \times 3 = 27$ possible ways to answer a 3-blank Text Completion—and only one of those 27 ways is correct. The guessing odds will go down, but don't be intimidated. Just follow the basic process: come up with your own filler for each blank, and match to the answer choices. If you're confused by this example, don't worry! We'll start from the beginning in our *Text Completion & Sentence Equivalence* strategy guide.

Strategy Tip: As on the old GRE, do NOT "write your own story." The GRE cannot give you a blank without also giving you a clue, physically written down in the passage, telling you what kind of word or phrase MUST go in that blank. Find that clue. You should be able to give textual evidence for each answer choice you select.

Verbal: Sentence Equivalence Questions

In this question type, you are given one sentence with a single blank. There are six answer choices, and you are asked to pick TWO choices that fit the blank and are alike in meaning.

Of the new question types, this one depends the most on vocabulary and also yields the most to strategy.

No partial credit is given on Sentence Equivalence; both correct answers must be selected. When you pick two of six choices, there are 15 possible combinations of choices, and only one is correct. However, this is not nearly as daunting as it sounds.

Think of it this way—if you have six choices, but the two correct ones must be "similar in meaning," then you have, at most, three possible PAIRS of choices. Maybe fewer, since not all choices are guaranteed to have a "partner." If you can match up the "pairs," you can seriously narrow down your options.

Here is a sample set of answer choices:

- [A] tractable
- [B] taciturn
- [C] arbitrary
- [D] tantamount
- [E] reticent
- [F] amenable

We haven't even given you the question here, because we want to point out how much you can do with the choices alone, if you have studied vocabulary sufficiently.

TRACTABLE and AMENABLE are synonyms (tractable, amenable people will do whatever you want them to do). TACITURN and RETICENT are synonyms (both mean "not talkative"). ARBITRARY (based on one's own will) and TANTAMOUT (equivalent) are not similar in meaning and therefore cannot be a pair. Therefore, the ONLY possible answers are {A, F} and {B, E}. We have improved our chances from 1 in 15 to a 50/50 shot without even reading the question!

Of course, in approaching a Sentence Equivalence, we do want to analyze the sentence the same way we would with a Text Completion—read for a textual clue that tells you what type of word MUST go in the blank. Then look for a matching pair.

Strategy Tip: If you're sure that a word in the choices does NOT have a partner, cross it out! For instance, if A and C are partners, and E and F are partners, and you're sure B and D are not each other's partners, cross out B and D completely. They cannot be the answer together, nor can either one be part of the answer.

The sentence for the answer choice above could read,

> Though the dinner guests were quite _____ , the hostess did her best to keep the conversation active and engaging.

Thus, B and E are the best choices. Let's try an example.

While athletes usually expect to achieve their greatest feats in their teens or twenties, opera singers don't reach the _____ of their vocal powers until middle age.

- [A] harmony
- [B] zenith
- [C] acme
- [D] terminus
- [E] nadir
- [F] cessation

Solution:

Those with strong vocabularies might go straight to the choices to make pairs. ZENITH and ACME are synonyms, meaning "high point, peak." TERMINUS and CESSATION are synonyms, meaning "end." NADIR is a low point and HARMONY is present here as a trap answer reminding us of opera singers. *Cross off A and E, since they do not have partners.* Then, go back to the sentence, knowing that your only options are a pair meaning "peak" and a pair meaning "end."

The answer is {B, C}.

Math: Quantitative Comparison

This format is a holdover from the old exam. Here's a quick example:

Quantity A   **Quantity B**

x x^2

(A) Quantity A is greater.
(B) Quantity B is greater.
(C) The two quantities are equal.
(D) The relationship cannot be determined from the information given.

Solution: If $x = 0$, the quantities are equal. If $x = 2$, quantity B is greater. Thus, we don't have enough information.

The answer is D.

Let's look at the new math question formats.

Math: Select One or More Answer Choices

According to the *Official Guide to the GRE Revised General Test*, the official directions for "Select One or More Answer Choices" read as follows:

> Directions: Select one or more answer choices according to the specific question directions.
>
> If the question does not specify how many answer choices to select, select all that apply.
>
> The correct answer may be just one of the choices or as many as all of the choices, depending on the question.
>
> No credit is given unless you select all of the correct choices and no others.
>
> If the question specifies how many answer choices to select, select exactly that number of choices.

Note that there is no "partial credit." If three of six choices are correct and you select two of the three, no credit is given. It will also be important to read the directions carefully.

That said, many of these questions look *very* similar to those on the "old" GRE. For instance, here is a question that could have appeared on the GRE in the past:

If $ab = |a| \times |b|$, which of the following *must* be true?

I.	$a = b$
II.	$a > 0$ and $b > 0$
III.	$ab > 0$

A.	II only
B.	III only
C.	I and III only
D.	II and III only
E.	I, II, and III

Solution: If $ab = |a| \times |b|$, then we know ab is positive, since the right side of the equation must be positive. If ab is positive, however, that doesn't necessarily mean that a and b are each positive; it simply means that they have the same sign.

I.	It is not true that a must equal b. For instance, a could be 2 and b could be 3.
II.	It is not true that a and b must each be positive. For instance, a could be −3 and b could be −4.
III.	True. Since $|a| \times |b|$ must be positive, ab must be positive as well.

The answer is B (III only).

Note that, if you determined that statement I was false, you could eliminate choices C and E before considering the remaining statements. Then, if you were confident that II was also false, you could safely pick answer choice B, III only, without even trying statement III, since "None of the above" isn't an option. That is, because of the multiple choice answers, it is sometimes not necessary to consider each statement individually. This is the aspect of such problems that will change on the new exam.

Here is the same problem, in the new format.

If $ab = |a| \times |b|$, which of the following *must* be true?

Indicate <u>all</u> such statements.

$\boxed{A}$	$a = b$
$\boxed{B}$	$a > 0$ and $b > 0$
$\boxed{C}$	$ab > 0$

Strategy Tip: Make sure to fully "process" the statement in the question (simplify it or list the possible scenarios) before considering the answer choices. This will save you time in the long run!

Here, we would simply select choice C. The only thing that has changed is that we can't do process of elimination; we must always consider each statement individually. On the upside, the problem has become much more straightforward and compact (not every real-life problem has exactly five possible solutions; why should those on the GRE?).

Math: Numeric Entry

This question type requires the text taker to key a numeric answer into a box on the screen. You are not able to "work backwards" from answer choices, and in many cases it will be difficult to make a guess. However, the principles being tested are the same as on the old GRE.

Here is a sample question:

If $x*y = 2xy - (x - y)$, what is the value of 3*4?

Solution:

We are given a function involving two variables, x and y, and asked to substitute 3 for x and 4 for y:

$$x*y = 2xy - (x - y)$$
$$3*4 = 2(3)(4) - (3 - 4)$$
$$3*4 = 24 - (-1)$$
$$3*4 = 25$$

The answer is 25.

Thus, you would type 25 into the box.

Okay. You've now got a good start on understanding the structure and question formats of the new GRE. Now it's time to begin fine-tuning your skills.

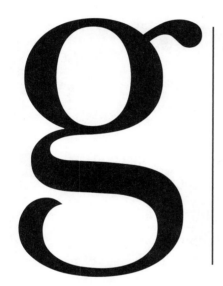

Chapter 2
of
NUMBER PROPERTIES

DIVISIBILITY &
PRIMES

In This Chapter . . .

- Divisibility Rules

- Factors

- Prime Numbers

- Prime Factorization

- The Factor Foundation Rule

- The Factor/Prime Factorization Connection

- Unknown Numbers and Divisibility

- Fewer Factors, More Multiples

- Divisibility and Addition/Subtraction

- Remainders

DIVISIBILITY

In This Chapter:

- Divisibility rules
- How to find the factors of a number
- The connection between factors and divisibility
- How to answer questions on the GRE related to divisibility

There is a category of problems on the GRE that tests what could broadly be referred to as "Number Properties." These questions are focused on a very important subset of numbers known as integers. Before we explore divisibility any further, it will be necessary to understand exactly what integers are and how they function.

Integers are whole numbers. That means that they are numbers that do not have any decimals or fractions attached. Some people think of them as counting numbers, i.e. 1, 2, 3... etc. Integers can be positive, and they can also be negative. −1, −2, −3... etc. are all integers as well. And there's one more important number that qualifies as an integer: 0.

So numbers such as 7, 15,003, −346, and 0 are all integers. Numbers such as 1.3, 3/4, and π are not integers.

Now that we know what integers are, let's see what we know about them when dealing with the four basic operations: addition, subtraction, multiplication and division.

integer + integer = always an integer	ex. $4 + 11 = 15$
integer − integer = always an integer	ex. $-5 - 32 = -37$
integer × integer = always an integer	ex. $14 \times 3 = 42$

None of these properties of integers turn out to be very interesting. But what happens when we *divide* an integer by another integer? Well, $18 \div 3 = 6$, which is an integer, but $12 \div 8 = 1.5$, which is not an integer.

If an integer divides another integer and the result, or quotient, is an integer, we say the first number is divisible by the second. So 18 is divisible by 3 because $18 \div 3 =$ an integer. On the other hand, we would say that 12 is NOT divisible by 8, because $12 \div 8$ is not an integer.

Divisibility Rules

The Divisibility Rules are important shortcuts to determine whether an integer is divisible by 2, 3, 4, 5, 6, 8, 9, and 10. You can always use your calculator to test divisibility, but these shortcuts will save you time.

An integer is divisible by:

2 if the integer is EVEN.
12 is divisible by 2, but 13 is not. Integers that are divisible by 2 are called "even" and integers that are not are called "odd." You can tell whether a number is even by checking to see whether the units (ones) digit is 0, 2, 4, 6, or 8. Thus, 1,234,567 is odd, because 7 is odd, whereas 2,345,678 is even, because 8 is even.

3 if the SUM of the integer's DIGITS is divisible by 3.
72 is divisible by 3 because the sum of its digits is 9, which is divisible by 3. By contrast, 83 is not divisible by 3, because the sum of its digits is 11, which is not divisible by 3.

4 if the integer is divisible by 2 TWICE, or if the LAST TWO digits are divisible by 4.

28 is divisible by 4 because you can divide it by 2 twice and get an integer result (28 ÷ 2 = 14, and 14 ÷ 2 = 7). For larger numbers, check only the last two digits. For example, 23,456 is divisible by 4 because 56 is divisible by 4, but 25,678 is not divisible by 4 because 78 is not divisible by 4.

5 if the integer ends in 0 or 5.

75 and 80 are divisible by 5, but 77 and 83 are not.

6 if the integer is divisible by BOTH 2 and 3.

48 is divisible by 6 since it is divisible by 2 (it ends with an 8, which is even) AND by 3 (4 + 8 = 12, which is divisible by 3).

8 if the integer is divisible by 2 THREE TIMES, or if the LAST THREE digits are divisible by 8.

32 is divisible by 8 since you can divide it by 2 three times and get an integer result (32 ÷ 2 = 16, 16 ÷ 2 = 8, and 8 ÷ 2 = 4). For larger numbers, check only the last 3 digits. For example, 23,456 is divisible by 8 because 456 is divisible by 8, whereas 23,556 is not divisible by 8 because 556 is not divisible by 8.

9 if the SUM of the integer's DIGITS is divisible by 9.

4,185 is divisible by 9 since the sum of its digits is 18, which is divisible by 9. By contrast, 3,459 is not divisible by 9, because the sum of its digits is 21, which is not divisible by 9.

10 if the integer ends in 0.

670 is divisible by 10, but 675 is not.

The GRE can also test these divisibility rules in reverse. For example, if you are told that a number has a ones digit equal to 0, you can infer that that number is divisible by 10. Similarly, if you are told that the sum of the digits of x is equal to 21, you can infer that x is divisible by 3 but NOT by 9.

Note also that there is no rule listed for divisibility by 7. The simplest way to check for divisibility by 7, or by any other number not found in this list, is to use the calculator.

Check Your Skills

1. Is 123,456,789 divisible by 2?
2. Is 732 divisible by 3?
3. Is 989 divisible by 9?
4. Is 4,578 divisible by 4?
5. Is 4,578 divisible by 6?
6. Is 603,864 divisible by 8?

Answers can be found on page 45.

Factors

Let's continue to explore the question of divisibility by asking the question, what numbers is 6 divisible by? Questions related to divisibility are only interested in positive integers, so we really only have 6 possible numbers: 1, 2, 3, 4, 5, and 6. So let's see which numbers 6 is divisible by.

$6 \div 1 = 6$	Any number divided by 1 equals itself, so an integer divided by 1 will be an integer.
$6 \div 2 = 3$	
$6 \div 3 = 2$	Note that these form a pair
$6 \div 4 = 1.5$	
$6 \div 5 = 1.2$	Not integers, so 6 is NOT divisible by 4 or by 5.
$6 \div 6 = 1$	Any number divided by itself equals 1, so an integer is always divisible by itself.

So 6 is divisible by 1, 2, 3 and 6. That means that 1, 2, 3 and 6 are **factors** of 6. There are a variety of ways you might see this relationship expressed on the GRE.

2 is a factor of 6	6 is a multiple of 2
2 is a divisor of 6	6 is divisible by 2
2 divides 6	2 goes into 6

Sometimes it will be necessary to find the factors of a number in order to answer a question. An easy way to find all the factors of a small number is to use factor pairs. Factor pairs for any integer are the pairs of factors that, when multiplied together, yield that integer.

Here's a step-by-step way to find all the factors of the number 60 using a **factor pairs table:**

(1) Make a table with 2 columns labeled "Small" and "Large."

(2) Start with 1 in the small column and 60 in the large column. (The first set of factor pairs will always be 1 and the number itself.)

(3) The next number after 1 is 2. If 2 is a factor of 60, then write "2" underneath the "1" in your table. It is, so divide 60 by 2 to find the factor pair: $60 \div 2 = 30$. Write "30" in the large column.

(4) The next number after 2 is 3. Repeat this process until the numbers in the small and the large columns run into each other. In this case, we find that 6 and 10 are a factor pair. But 7, 8 and 9 are not factors of 60, and the next number after 9 is 10, which appears in the large column, so we can stop.

Small	Large
1	60
2	30
3	20
4	15
5	12
6	10

The advantage of using this method, as opposed to thinking of factors and listing them out, is that this is an organized, methodical approach that makes it easier to find every factor of a number quickly. Let's practice. (This is also a good opportunity to practice your long division.)

Check Your Skills

7. Find all the factors of 90.
8. Find all the factors of 72.
9. Find all the factors of 105.
10. Find all the factors of 120.

Answers can be found on pages 45–46.

Prime Numbers

Let's backtrack a little bit and try finding the factors of another small number: 7. Our only possibilities are the positive integers less than or equal to 7, so let's check every possibility.

$7 \div 1 = 7$ Every number is divisible by 1—no surprise there!

$7 \div 2 = 3.5$

$7 \div 3 = 2.33...$

$7 \div 4 = 1.75$ 7 is not divisible by *any* integer besides 1 and itself

$7 \div 5 = 1.4$

$7 \div 6 = 1.16...$

$7 \div 7 = 1$ Every number is divisible by itself—boring!

So 7 only has two factors—1 and itself. Numbers that only have 2 factors are known as **prime numbers.** As we will see, prime numbers play a very important role in answering questions about divisibility. Because they're so important, it's critical that we learn to identify what numbers are prime and what numbers aren't.

The prime numbers that appear most frequently on the test are prime numbers less than 20. They are 2, 3, 5, 7, 11, 13, 17 and 19. Two things to note about this list: 1 is not prime, and out of *all* the prime numbers, 2 is the *only* even prime number.

2 is prime because it has only two factors—1 and itself. The reason that it's the only even prime number is that *every* even number is divisible by 2, and thus has another factor besides 1 and itself. For instance, we can immediately tell that 12,408 isn't prime, because we know that it has at least one factor besides 1 and itself: 2.

So every positive integer can be placed into one of two categories—prime or not prime.

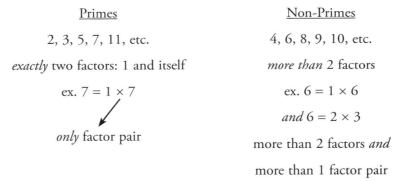

Primes	Non-Primes
2, 3, 5, 7, 11, etc.	4, 6, 8, 9, 10, etc.
exactly two factors: 1 and itself	*more than* 2 factors
ex. 7 = 1 × 7	ex. 6 = 1 × 6
	and 6 = 2 × 3
only factor pair	more than 2 factors *and*
	more than 1 factor pair

Check Your Skills

11. List all the prime numbers between 20 and 50.

The answer can be found on page 46.

Prime Factorization

Let's take another look at 60. When we found the factor pairs of 60, we discovered that it had 12 factors and 6 factor pairs.

$60 = 1 \times 60$ Always the first factor pair—boring!

and 2×30

and 3×20

and 4×15 5 other factor pairs—interesting!
                          Let's look at these in a little more detail.
and 5×12

and 6×10

From here on, we will be referring to boring and interesting factor pairs. These are not technical terms, but the boring factor pair is the factor pair that involves 1 and the number itself. All other pairs are interesting pairs. Keep reading to see why!

Let's look at one of these factor pairs—4×15. One way to think about this pair is that 60 *breaks down* into 4 and 15. One way to express this relationship visually is to use a **factor tree.**

Now, the question arises—can we go further? Sure! Neither 4 nor 15 is prime, which means they both have factor pairs that we might find *interesting*. 4 breaks down into 2×2, and 15 breaks down into 3×5:

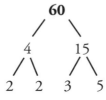

Can we break it down any further? Not with *interesting* factor pairs. We could say that $2 = 2 \times 1$, for instance, but that doesn't provide us any new information. The reason we can't go any further is that 2, 2, 3 and 5 are all *prime numbers*. Prime numbers only have one boring factor pair. So when we find a prime factor, we know that that branch of our factor tree has reached its end. We can go one step further and circle every prime number as we go, reminding us that we can't break down that branch any further. The factor tree for 60 would look like this:

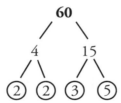

So after we broke down 60 into 4 and 15, and broke 4 and 15 down, we ended up with $60 = 2 \times 2 \times 3 \times 5$.

What if we start with a different factor pair of 60? Let's create a factor tree for 60 in which the first breakdown we make is 6 × 10.

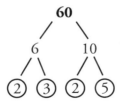

According to this factor tree 60 = 2 × 3 × 2 × 5. Notice that, even though they're in a different order, this is the same group of prime numbers we had before. In fact, *any* way we break down 60, we will end up with the same prime factors: two 2's, one 3 and one 5. Another way to say this is that 2 × 2 × 3 × 5 is the **prime factorization** of 60.

One way to think about prime factors is that they are the DNA of a number. Every number has a unique prime factorization. 60 is the only number that can be written as 2 × 2 × 3 × 5. Breaking down numbers into their prime factors is the key to answering many divisibility problems.

As we proceed through the chapter, we'll discuss what prime factors can tell us about a number and some different types of questions the GRE may ask. But because the prime factorization of a number is so important, first we need a fast, reliable way to find the prime factorization of *any* number.

A factor tree is the best way to find the prime factorization of a number. A number like 60 should be relatively straightforward to break down into primes, but what if you need the prime factorization of 630?

For large numbers, it's often best to start with the smallest prime factors and work your way toward larger primes. This is why it's good to know your divisibility rules!

Take a second to try on your own, and then we'll go through it together.

Start by finding the smallest prime number that 630 is divisible by. The smallest prime number is 2. 630 is even, so we know it must be divisible by 2. 630 divided by 2 is 315, so our first breakdown of 630 is into 2 and 315.

Now we still need to factor 315. It's not even, so we know it's not divisible by 2. Is it divisible by 3? If the digits of 315 add up to a multiple of 3, it is. 3 + 1 + 5 = 9, which is a multiple of 3, so 315 is divisible by 3. 315 divided by 3 is 105, so our factor tree now looks like this:

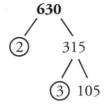

If 315 was not divisible by 2, then 105 won't be either (we will discuss why later), but 105 might still be divisible by 3. 1 + 0 + 5 = 6, so 105 is divisible by 3. 105 ÷ 3 = 35, so our tree now looks like this:

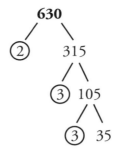

35 is not divisible by 3 (3 + 5 = 8, which is not a multiple of 3), so the next number to try is 5. 35 ends in a 5, so we know it is divisible by 5. 35 ÷ 5 = 7, so our tree now looks like this:

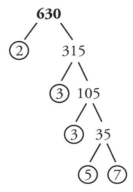

Every number on the tree has now been broken down as far as it can go. So the prime factorization of 630 is 2 × 3 × 3 × 5 × 7.

Alternatively, you could have split 630 into 63 and 10, since it's easy to see that 630 is divisible by 10. Then you would proceed from there. Either way will get you to the same set of prime factors.

Now it's time to get a little practice doing prime factorizations.

Check Your Skills

12. Find the prime factorization of 90.
13. Find the prime factorization of 72.
14. Find the prime factorization of 105.
15. Find the prime factorization of 120.

Answers can be found on pages 46–47.

The Factor Foundation Rule

This discussion begins with the **factor foundation rule.** The factor foundation rule states that if a is divisible by b, and b is divisible by c, then a is divisible by c as well. In other words, if we know that 12 is divisible by 6, and 6 is divisible by 3, then 12 is divisible by 3 as well.

This rule also works in reverse to a certain extent. If d is divisible by two different primes, e and f, d is also divisible by $e \times f$. In other words, if 20 is divisible by 2 and by 5, then 20 is also divisible by 2 × 5 (10).

Another way to think of this rule is that divisibility travels up and down the factor tree. Let's walk through the factor tree of 150. We'll break it down, and then we'll build it back up.

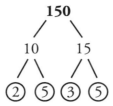

150 is divisible by 10 and by 15, so 150 is also divisible by *everything* that 10 and 15 are divisible by. 10 is divisible by 2 and 5, so 150 is also divisible by 2 and 5. 15 is divisible by 3 and 5, so 150 is also divisible by 3 and 5. Taken all together, we know that the prime factorization of 150 is 2 × 3 × 5 × 5. We could represent that information like this:

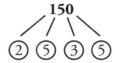

Think of prime factors as building blocks. In the case of 150, we have one 2, one 3 and two 5's at our disposal to build other factors of 150. In our first example, we went down the tree —from 150 down to 10 and 15, and then down again to 2, 5, 3 and 5. But we can also build upwards, starting with our four building blocks. For instance, 2 × 3 = 6, and 5 × 5 = 25, so our tree could also look like this:

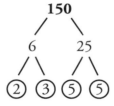

(Even though 5 and 5 are not different primes, 5 appears twice on 150's tree. So we are allowed to multiply those two 5's together to produce another factor of 150, namely 25.)

The tree above isn't even the only other possibility. These are all trees that we could build using different combinations of our prime factors.

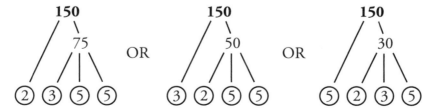

We began with four prime factors of 150: 2, 3, 5 and 5. But we were able to build different factors by multiplying 2, 3 or even all 4 of those primes together in different combinations. As it turns out, *all* of the factors of a number (except for 1) can be built with different combinations of its prime factors.

The Factor/Prime Factorization Connection

Let's take one more look at the number 60 and its factors. Specifically, let's look at the prime factorizations of all the factors of 60.

	Small	Large	
1	1	60	$2 \times 2 \times 3 \times 5$
2	2	30	$2 \times 3 \times 5$
3	3	20	$2 \times 2 \times 5$
2×2	4	15	3×5
5	5	12	$2 \times 2 \times 3$
2×3	6	10	2×5

All the factors of 60 are just different combinations of the prime numbers that make up the prime factorization of 60. To say this another way, every factor of a number can be expressed as the product of a combination of its prime factors. Take a look back at your work for Check Your Skills questions 7–10 and 12–15. Break down all the factor pairs from the first section into their prime factors. This relationship between factors and prime factors is true of every number.

Now that you know why prime factors are so important, it's time for the next step. An important skill on the GRE is to take the given information in a question and go further with it. For example, if a question tells you that a number *n* is even, what else do you know about it? Every even number is a multiple of 2, so *n* is a multiple of 2. These kinds of inferences often provide crucial information necessary to correctly solving problems.

So far, we've been finding factors and prime factors of numbers—but the GRE will sometimes ask divisibility questions about *variables*. In the next section, we'll take our discussion of divisibility to the next level and bring variables into the picture. But first, we'll recap what we've learned so far and what tools we'll need going forward.

1. If *a* is divisible by *b*, and *b* is divisible by *c*, then *a* is divisible by *c* as well. (ex. 100 is divisible by 20, and 20 is divisible by 4, so 100 is divisible by 4 as well.)

2. If *d* has *e* and *f* as prime factors, *d* is also divisible by $e \times f$. (ex. 90 is divisible by 5 and by 3, so 90 is also divisible by $5 \times 3 = 15$.) You can let *e* and *f* be the same prime, as long as there are at least 2 copies of that prime in *d*'s factor tree.

3. Every factor of a number (except 1) is either prime or the product of a different combination of that number's prime factors. For example, $30 = 2 \times 3 \times 5$. Its factors are 1, 2, 3, 5, 6 (2×3), 10 (2×5), 15 (3×5) and 30 ($2 \times 3 \times 5$). (ex. 98 has two 7's in its factors, and so is divisible by 49.)

4. To find *all* the factors of a number in an easy, methodical way, set up a factor pairs table.

5. To find *all* the prime factors of a number, use a factor tree. With larger numbers, start with the smallest primes and work your way up to larger primes.

Check Your Skills

16. The prime factorization of a number is 3×5. What is the number and what are all its factors?
17. The prime factorization of a number is $2 \times 5 \times 7$. What is the number and what are all its factors?
18. The prime factorization of a number is $2 \times 3 \times 13$. What is the number and what are all its factors?

Answers can be found on pages 47–48.

Unknown Numbers and Divisibility

Let's say that you are told some unknown positive number x is divisible by 6. How can you represent this on paper? There are many ways, depending on the problem. You could say that you know that x is a multiple of 6, or you could say that $x = 6 \times$ an integer. You could also represent the information with a factor tree. Careful though— although we've had a lot of practice drawing factor trees, there is one important difference now that we're dealing with an unknown number. We know that x is divisible by 6, but x may be divisible by other numbers as well. We have to treat what they have told us as incomplete information, and remind ourselves there are other things about x we don't know. To represent that on the page, our factor tree could look like this:

Now the question becomes—what else do we know about x? If a question on the GRE told you that x is divisible by 6, what could you definitely say about x? Take a look at these three statements, and for each statement, decide whether it *must* be true, whether it *could* be true, or whether it *cannot* be true.

   I. x is divisible by 3

   II. x is even

   III x is divisible by 12

We'll deal with each statement one at a time. Let's begin with statement I—x is divisible by 3. One approach to take here is to think about the multiples of 6. If x is divisible by 6, then we know that x is a multiple of 6. Let's list out the first several multiples of 6, and see if they're divisible by 3.

	6	$6 \div 12 = 0.5$
	12	$12 \div 12 = 1$
x is a number on this list	18	$18 \div 12 = 1.5$
	24	$24 \div 12 = 2$
	…	…

Some, but not all, of these numbers are also divisible by 12.

At this point, we can be fairly certain that x is divisible by 3. In fact, listing out possible values of a variable is often a great way to begin answering a question in which you don't know the value of the number you are asked about.

But can we do better than say we're fairly certain x is divisible by 3? Is there a way to definitively say x *must* be divisible by 3? As it turns out, there is. Let's return to our factor tree, but let's make one modification to it.

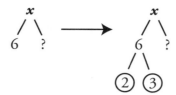

Remember, the ultimate purpose of the factor tree is to break numbers down into their fundamental building blocks: prime numbers. Now that the factor tree is broken down as far as it will go, we can apply the factor foundation rule. x is divisible by 6, and 6 is divisible by 3, so we can say definitively that x *must* be divisible by 3.

In fact, questions like this one are the reason we spent so much time discussing the factor foundation rule and the connection between prime factors and divisibility. Prime factors provide the foundation for a way to make definite statements about divisibility. With that in mind, let's look at statement II.

Statement II says x is even. This question is about divisibility, so the question becomes, what is the connection between divisibility and a number being even? Remember, an important part of this test is the ability to make inferences based on the given information.

What's the connection? Well, being even means being divisible by 2. So if we know that x is divisible by 2, then we can guarantee that x is even. Let's return to our factor tree.

We can once again make use of the factor foundation rule—6 is divisible by 2, so we know that x *must* be divisible by 2 as well. And if x is divisible by 2, then we know that x *must* be even as well.

That just leaves the final statement. Statement III says x is divisible by 12. Let's look at this question from the perspective of factor trees. Let's compare the factor tree of x with the factor tree of 12.

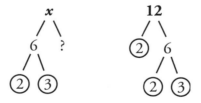

What would we have to know about x to guarantee that it is divisible by 12? Well, when 12 is broken down all the way, we see that 12 is $2 \times 2 \times 3$. 12's building blocks are two 2's and a 3. For x to be divisible by 12, it would have to also have two 2's and one 3 among its prime factors. In other words, for x to be divisible by 12, it has to be divisible by *everything* that 12 is divisible by.

We need x to be divisible by two 2's and one 3 in order to say it *must* be divisible by 12. But looking at our factor tree, we only see one 2 and one 3. Because there is only one 2, we can't say that x *must* be divisible by 12. But then the question becomes, *could* x be divisible by 12? Think about the question for a second, and then keep reading.

The key to this question is the question mark that we put on *x*'s factor tree. That question mark reminds us that we don't know everything about *x*. *x* could have other prime factors. What if one of those unknown factors was another 2? Then our tree would look like this:

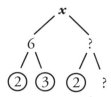

So *if* one of those unknown factors were a 2, then *x* would be divisible by 12. The key here is that we have no way of knowing for sure whether there is a 2. *x* may be divisible by 12, it may not. In other words, *x could* be divisible by 12.

To confirm this, we can go back to the multiples of 6. We still know that *x* must be a multiple of 6, so let's start by listing out the first several multiples and see if they are divisible by 12.

x is a number on this list	6	$6 \div 3 = 2$	All of these numbers are also divisible by 3.
	12	$12 \div 3 = 4$	
	18	$18 \div 3 = 6$	
	24	$24 \div 3 = 8$	
	...	...	

Once again, we see that some of the possible values of *x* are divisible by 12, and some aren't. The best we can say is that *x could* be divisible by 12.

Check Your Skills

For these statements, the following is true: *x* is divisible by 24. For each statement, say whether it *must* be true, *could* be true, or *cannot* be true.

19. *x* is divisible by 6
20. *x* is divisible by 9
21. *x* is divisible by 8

Answers can be found on pages 48–49.

Let's answer another question, this time with an additional twist. Once again, there will be three statements. Decide whether each statement *must* be true, *could* be true, or *cannot* be true. Answer this question on your own, then we'll discuss each statement one at a time on the next page.

    x is divisible by 3 and by 10.

        I. *x* is divisible by 2

        II. *x* is divisible by 15

        III. *x* is divisible by 45

Before we dive into the statements, let's spend a moment to organize the information the question has given us. We know that *x* is divisible by 3 and by 10, so we can create two factor trees to represent this information.

Now that we have our trees, let's get started with statement I. Statement I says that *x* is divisible by 2. The way to determine whether this statement is true should be fairly familiar by now—we need to use the factor foundation rule. First of all, our factor trees aren't quite finished. Factor trees should always be broken down all the way until every branch ends in a prime number. Really, our factor trees should look like this:

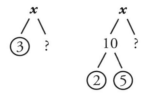

Now we are ready to decide whether statement I is true. *x* is divisible by 10, and 10 is divisible by 2, so we know that *x* is divisible by 2. Statement I *must* be true.

That brings us to statement II. This statement is a little more difficult. It also requires us to take another look at our factor trees. We have two separate trees, but they're giving us information about the same variable—*x*. Neither tree gives us complete information about *x*, but we do know a couple of things with absolute certainty. From the first tree, we know that *x* is divisible by 3, and from the second tree we know that *x* is divisible by 10—which really means we know that *x* is divisible by 2 and by 5. We can actually combine those two pieces of information and represent them on one factor tree.

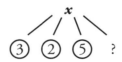

Now we know three prime factors of *x*: 2, 3 and 5. Let's return to the statement. Statement II says that *x* is divisible by 15. What do we need to know to say that *x* *must* be divisible by 15? If we can guarantee that *x* has all the prime factors that 15 has, then we can guarantee that *x* is divisible by 15.

15 breaks down into the prime factors 3 and 5. So to guarantee that *x* is divisible by 15, we need to know it's divisible by 3 and 5. Looking back up at our factor tree, we see that *x* has both a 3 and a 5, which means that we know *x* is divisible by 15. Therefore, statement II *must* be true.

We can also look at this question more visually. Remember, prime factors are like building blocks—we also know that *x* is divisible by any combination of these prime factors. We can combine the prime factors in a number of different ways.

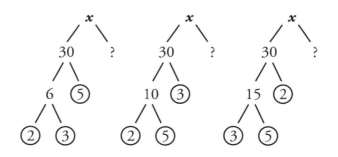

Each of these factor trees can tell us different factors of *x*. But what's really important is what they have in common. No matter what way you combine the prime factors, each tree ultimately leads to $2 \times 3 \times 5$, which equals 30. So we know that *x* is divisible by 30. And if *x* is divisible by 30, it is also divisible by everything 30 is divisible by. We know how to identify every number 30 is divisible by—we can use a factor pair table. The factor pair table of 30 looks like this.

Small	Large
1	30
2	15
3	10
5	6

Again, statement II says that *x* is divisible by 15. We know *x* is divisible by 30, and 30 is divisible by 15, so *x* *must* be divisible by 15.

That brings us to statement III. Statement III says that *x* is divisible by 45. What do we need to know to say that *x* *must* be divisible by 45? Build a factor tree of 45, which looks like this.

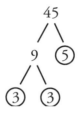

45 is divisible by 3, 3 and 5. For *x* to be divisible by 45, we need to know that it has all the same prime factors. Does it?

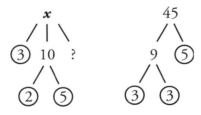

45 has one 5 and two 3's. We know that *x* has a 5, but we only know that *x* has one 3. That means that we can't say for sure that *x* is divisible by 45. *x could* be divisible by 45, because we don't know what the question mark contains. If it contains a 3, then *x* is divisible by 45. If it doesn't contain a 3, then *x* is not divisible by 45. Without more information, we can't say for sure either way. So statement III *could* be true.

Now it's time to recap what we've covered in this chapter. When we deal with questions about divisibility, we need a quick, accurate way to identify *all* the factors of a number. A factor pair table provides a reliable way to make sure you find every factor of a number.

Prime factors provide essential information about a number or variable. They are the fundamental building blocks of every number. In order for a number or variable to be divisible by another number, it must contain all the same prime factors that the other number contains. In our last example, we could definitely say that *x* was divisible by 15, because *x* contained a 3 and a 5. But we could not say that it was divisible by 45, because 45 has a 5 and two 3's, but *x* only had a 5 and one 3.

Check Your Skills

For these statements, the following is true: *x* is divisible by 28 and by 15. For each statement, say whether it *must* be true, *could* be true, or *cannot* be true.

22. *x* is divisible by 14.
23. *x* is divisible by 20.
24. *x* is divisible by 24.

Answers can be found on page 49–50.

Fewer Factors, More Multiples

Sometimes it is easy to confuse factors and multiples. The mnemonic "Fewer Factors, More Multiples" should help you remember the difference. Factors divide into an integer and are therefore less than or equal to that integer. Positive multiples, on the other hand, multiply out from an integer and are therefore greater than or equal to that integer.

Any integer only has a limited number of factors. For example, there are only four factors of 8: 1, 2, 4, and 8. By contrast, there is an infinite number of multiples of an integer. For example, the first 5 positive multiples of 8 are 8, 16, 24, 32, and 40, but you could go on listing multiples of 8 forever.

Factors, multiples, and divisibility are very closely related concepts. For example, 3 is a factor of 12. This is the same as saying that 12 is a multiple of 3, or that 12 is divisible by 3.

On the GRE, this terminology is often used interchangeably in order to make the problem seem harder than it actually is. Be aware of the different ways that the GRE can phrase information about divisibility. Moreover, try to convert all such statements to the same terminology. For example, **all** of the following statements **say exactly the same thing**:

- 12 is divisible by 3
- 12 is a multiple of 3
- $\dfrac{12}{3}$ is an integer
- 12 = 3*n*, where *n* is an integer
- 12 items can be shared among 3 people so that each person has the same number of items.

- 3 is a divisor of 12, or 3 is a factor of 12
- 3 divides 12
- $\dfrac{12}{3}$ yields a remainder of 0
- 3 "goes into" 12 evenly

Divisibility and Addition/Subtraction

If you add two multiples of 7, you get another multiple of 7. Try it: 35 + 21 = 56. This should make sense: (5 × 7) + (3 × 7) = (5 + 3) × 7 = 8 × 7.

Likewise, if you subtract two multiples of 7, you get another multiple of 7. Try it: 35 − 21 = 14. Again, we can see why: (5 × 7) − (3 × 7) = (5 − 3) × 7 = 2 × 7.

This pattern holds true for the multiples of any integer *N*. **If you add or subtract multiples of *N*, the result is a multiple of *N*.** You can restate this principle using any of the disguises above: for instance, if *N* is a divisor of *x* and of *y*, then *N* is a divisor of *x* + *y*.

Remainders

The number 17 is not divisible by 5. When you divide 17 by 5, using long division, you get a **remainder:** a number left over. In this case, the remainder is 2.

$$\begin{array}{r} 3 \\ 5\overline{)17} \\ -15 \\ \hline 2 \end{array}$$

We can also write that 17 is 2 more than 15, or 2 more than a multiple of 5. In other words, we can write $17 = 15 + 2 = 3 \times 5 + 2$. Every number that leaves a remainder of 2 after it is divided by 5 can be written this way: as a multiple of 5, plus 2.

On simpler remainder problems, it is often easiest to pick numbers. Simply add the desired remainder to a multiple of the divisor. For instance, if you need a number that leaves a remainder of 4 after division by 7, first pick a multiple of 7: say, 14. Then add 4 to get 18, which satisfies the requirement ($18 = 7 \times 2 + 4$).

A remainder is defined as the integer portion of the **dividend** (or numerator) that is not evenly divisible by the **divisor** (or denominator). Here is an example written in fractional notation:

$$\text{Dividend} \longrightarrow \frac{23}{4} = 5 + \frac{3}{4} \longleftarrow \text{Remainder}$$
$$\text{Divisor} \longrightarrow \qquad \uparrow \qquad \text{Quotient}$$

The **quotient** is the resulting integer portion that CAN be divided out (in this case, the quotient is 5). Note that the dividend, divisor, quotient and remainder will ALWAYS be integers. Sometimes, the quotient may be zero! For instance, when 3 is divided by 5, the remainder is 3 but the quotient is 0 (because 0 is the biggest multiple of 5 that can be divided out of 3).

Algebraically, this relationship can be written as the Remainder Formula:

$$\text{Dividend} \longrightarrow \frac{x}{N} = Q + \frac{R}{N} \longleftarrow \text{Remainder}$$
$$\text{Divisor} \longrightarrow \qquad \uparrow \qquad \text{Quotient}$$

This framework is often easiest to use on GRE problems when you multiply through by the divisor N:

$$\text{Dividend} \longrightarrow x = Q \cdot N + R \longleftarrow \text{Remainder}$$
$$\text{Quotient} \longrightarrow \qquad \uparrow \qquad \uparrow \qquad \text{Divisor}$$

(Example: $23 = 5 \times 4 + 3$)

Again, remember that x, Q, N, and R must ALL be integers. It should <u>also</u> be noted that R must be equal to or greater than 0, but less than N (the divisor). This is discussed below.

Range of Possible Remainders

When you divide an integer by 7, the remainder could be 0, 1, 2, 3, 4, 5, or 6. Notice that you cannot have a negative remainder or a remainder larger than 7, and that you have exactly 7 possible remainders. You can see these remainders repeating themselves on the Remainder Ruler:

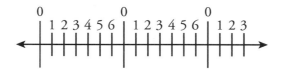

This pattern can be generalized. When you divide an integer by a positive integer N, the possible remainders range from 0 to $(N-1)$. There are thus N possible remainders. Negative remainders are not possible, nor are remainders equal to or larger than N.

> If $a \div b$ yields a remainder of 3, $c \div d$ yields a remainder of 4, and a, b, c and d are all integers, what is the smallest possible value for $b + d$?

Since the remainder must be smaller than the divisor, 3 must be smaller than b. b must be an integer, so b is at least 4. Similarly, 4 must be smaller than d, and d must be an integer, so d must be at least 5. Therefore the smallest possible value for $b + d$ is $4 + 5 = 9$.

Remainder of 0

If x divided by y yields a remainder of 0 (commonly referred to as "no remainder"), then x is divisible by y. Conversely, if x is divisible by y, then x divided by y yields a remainder of 0 (or "no remainder").

Similarly, if x divided by y yields a remainder greater than 0, then x is NOT divisible by y, and vice versa.

Arithmetic with Remainders

Two useful tips for arithmetic with remainders, if you have the same divisor throughout:

(1) You can add and subtract remainders directly, as long as you correct excess or negative remainders.
"Excess remainders" are remainders larger than or equal to the divisor. To correct excess or negative remainders, just add or subtract the divisor. For instance, if x leaves a remainder of 4 after division by 7, and y leaves a remainder of 2 after division by 7, then $x + y$ leaves a remainder of $4 + 2 = 6$ after division by 7. You do not need to pick numbers or write algebraic expressions for x and y. We can simply write R4 + R2 = R6.

If x leaves a remainder of 4 after division by 7 and z leaves a remainder of 5 after division by 7, then adding the remainders together yields 9. This number is too high, however. The remainder must be non-negative and less than 7. We can take an additional 7 out of the remainder, because 7 is the **excess** portion. The correct remainder is thus R4 + R5 = R9 = R2 (subtracting 7 out).

With the same x and z, subtraction of the remainders gives −1, which is also an unacceptable remainder (it must be non-negative). In this case, add an extra 7 to see that $x - z$ leaves a remainder of 6 after division by 7. Using R's, we can write R4 − R5 = R(−1) = R6 (adding a 7 in).

(2) You can multiply remainders, as long as you correct excess remainders at the end.

Again, if x has a remainder of 4 upon division by 7 and z has a remainder of 5 upon division by 7, then 4×5 gives 20. Two additional 7's can be taken out of this remainder, so $x \times z$ will have remainder 6 upon division by 7. In other words, (R4)(R5) = R20 = R6 (taking out two 7's). We can prove this by again picking $x = 25$ and $z = 12$ (try the algebraic method on your own!):

$$25 \times 12 = 300 = 42 \times 7 + 6 \longleftarrow \textbf{Remainder}$$

Quotient ⟶   **Divisor**

Check Your Skills

25. What is the remainder when 13 is divided by 6?

26. What's the first double-digit number that results in a remainder of 4 when divided by 5?

27. If x has a remainder of 4 when divided by 9 and y has a remainder of 3 when divided by 9, what's the remainder when $x + y$ is divided by 9?

28. Using this example, what's the remainder when xy is divided by 9?

Answers can be found on page 50.

Check Your Skills Answer Key:

1.   Is 123,456,789 divisible by 2?

123,456,789 is an odd number, because it ends in 9. So 123,456,789 is not divisible by 2.

2.   Is 732 divisible by 3?

The digits of 732 add up to a multiple of 3 ($7 + 3 + 2 = 12$). 732 is divisible by 3.

3.   Is 989 divisible by 9?

The digits of 989 do not add up to a multiple of 9 ($9 + 8 + 9 = 26$). 989 is not divisible by 9.

4. **No:** Any number whose last two digits are divisible by 4 is divisible by 4. 78 is not divisible by 4, so 4,578 is not divisible by 4.

5. **Yes:** Any number divisible by both 2 and 3 is divisible by 6. 4,578 must be divisible by 2, because it ends in an even number. It also must be divisible by 3, because the sum of its digits is a multiple of 3 ($4 + 5 + 7 + 8 = 24$). Therefore 4,578 is divisible by 6.

6. **Yes:** Easiest to use your calculator for this one! $603,864 \div 8 = 75,483$ with no remainder.

7.   Find all the factors of 90.

Small	Large
1	90
2	45
3	30
5	18
6	15
9	10

8.   Find all the factors of 72.

Small	Large
1	72
2	36
3	24
4	18
6	12
8	9

9.   Find all the factors of 105.

Small	Large
1	105
3	35
5	21
7	15

10.   Find all the factors of 120.

Small	Large
1	120
2	60
3	40
4	30
5	24
6	20
8	15
10	12

11.   List all the prime numbers between 20 and 50.

23, 29, 31, 37, 41, 43, and 47.

12.   Find the prime factorization of 90.

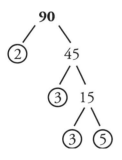

13.   Find the prime factorization of 72.

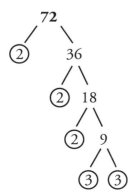

14.   Find the prime factorization of 105.

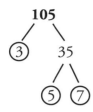

15.   Find the prime factorization of 120.

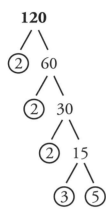

16.   The prime factorization of a number is 3×5. What is the number and what are all its factors?

$3 \times 5 = 15$

Small	Large
1	15
3	5

17.   The prime factorization of a number is $2 \times 5 \times 7$. What is the number and what are all its factors?

$2 \times 5 \times 7 = 70$

	Small	Large	
1	1	70	$2 \times 5 \times 7$
2	2	35	5×7
5	5	14	2×7
7	7	10	2×5

18.   The prime factorization of a number is $2 \times 3 \times 13$. What is the number and what are all its factors?

$2 \times 3 \times 13 = 78$

	Small	Large	
1	1	78	$2 \times 3 \times 13$
2	2	39	3×13
3	3	26	2×13
2×3	6	13	13

For questions 19–21, x is divisible by 24.

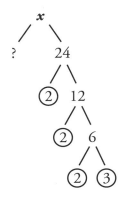

19. x is divisible by 6

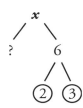

For x to be divisible by 6, we need to know that it contains the same prime factors as 6. 6 contains a 2 and a 3. x also contains a 2 and a 3, therefore x *must* be divisible by 6.

20. x is divisible by 9

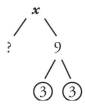

For x to be divisible by 9, we need to know that it contains the same prime factors as 9. 9 contains two 3's. x only contains one 3 that we know of. But the question mark means x may have other prime factors, and may contain another 3. For this reason, x *could* be divisible by 9.

21. *x* is divisible by 8

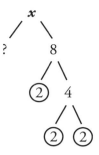

For *x* to be divisible by 8, we need to know that it contains the same prime factors as 8. 8 contains three 2's. *x* also contains three 2's, therefore *x* *must* be divisible by 8.

For questions 22–24, x is divisible by 28 and by 15.

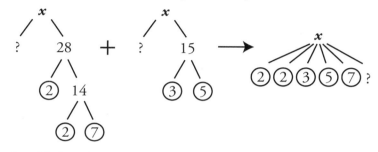

22. *x* is divisible by 14.

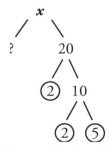

For *x* to be divisible by 14, we need to know that it contains the same prime factors as 14. 14 contains a 2 and a 7. *x* also contains a 2 and a 7, therefore *x* *must* be divisible by 14.

23. *x* is divisible by 20.

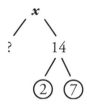

For *x* to be divisible by 20, we need to know that it contains the same prime factors as 20. 20 contains two 2's and a 5. *x* also contains two 2's and a 5, therefore *x* *must* be divisible by 20.

24. *x* is divisible by 24.

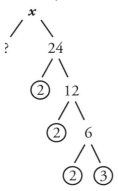

For *x* to be divisible by 24, we need to know that it contains the same prime factors as 24. 24 contains three 2's and a 3. *x* contains a 3, but only two 2's that we know of. But the question mark means *x* may have other prime factors, and may contain another 2. For this reason, *x could* be divisible by 24.

25. **1:** 6 goes into 13 two full times, which means the quotient is 2. 2 × 6 = 12, and 12 + 1 = 13. The remainder is 1.

26. **14:** For a number to result in a remainder of 4 when divided by 5, it has to be equal to a multiple of 5, plus 4. The first of these is 4 (5 × 0 + 4 = 4), the second is 9 (5 × 1 + 4 = 9), and the third is 14 (5 × 2 + 4). 14 is the first double-digit number that gets you the required remainder.

27. **7:** Using the Remainder Formula:

$$\frac{x}{9} = Q + \frac{4}{9} \rightarrow x = 9Q + 4$$
$$\frac{y}{9} = Q' + \frac{3}{9} \rightarrow y = 9Q' + 3$$

Therefore *x* + *y* = 9 (*Q* + *Q'*) + 7 and the remainder is 7.

28. **3:** Again using the Remainder Formula:

$$\frac{x}{9} = Q + \frac{4}{9} \rightarrow x = 9Q + 4$$
$$\frac{y}{9} = Q' + \frac{3}{9} \rightarrow y = 9Q' + 3$$

Therefore *xy* = (9*Q* + 4)(9*Q'* + 3) = 81*QQ'* + 27*Q* + 36*Q'* + 12.

Since a 9 can be removed from 12, the correct answer is 12 − 9 = 3.

*Manhattan*GRE˚ Prep
the new standard

Problem Set

For problems #1–10, use prime factorization, if appropriate, to answer each question: YES, NO, or CANNOT BE DETERMINED. If your answer is CANNOT BE DETERMINED, use two numerical examples to show how the problem could go either way. All variables in problems #1 through #12 are assumed to be integers unless otherwise indicated.

1.   If a is divided by 7 or by 18, an integer results. Is $\dfrac{a}{42}$ an integer?

2.   If 80 is a factor of r, is 15 a factor of r?

3.   Given that 7 is a factor of n and 7 is a factor of p, is $n + p$ divisible by 7?

4.   Given that 8 is not a factor of g, is 8 a factor of $2g$?

5.   If j is divisible by 12 and 10, is j divisible by 24?

6.   If 12 is a factor of xyz, is 12 a factor of xy?

7.   Given that 6 is a divisor of r and r is a factor of s, is 6 a factor of s?

8.   If 24 is a factor of h and 28 is a factor of k, must 21 be a factor of hk?

9.   If 6 is not a factor of d, is $12d$ divisible by 6?

10.   If 60 is a factor of u, is 18 a factor of u?

11.

Quantity A	**Quantity B**
The number of distinct prime factors in 40	The number of distinct prime factors in 50

12.

Quantity A	**Quantity B**
The product of 12 and an even prime number	The sum of the greatest four factors of 12

13.

$$x = 20, \ y = 32 \text{ and } z = 12$$

Quantity A	**Quantity B**
The remainder when x is divided by z	The remainder when y is divided by z

14. If $\dfrac{a}{b}$ has a remainder of 4, what is the smallest possible value of $a + b$?

15. If $\dfrac{x}{y}$ has a remainder of 0 and $\dfrac{z}{y}$ has a remainder of 3, what is the remainder of $\dfrac{xz}{y}$?

1. **YES:**

If *a* is divisible by 7 and by 18, its prime factors include 2, 3, 3, and 7, as indicated by the factor tree to the right. Therefore, any integer that can be constructed as a product of any of these prime factors is also a factor of *a*. $42 = 2 \times 3 \times 7$. Therefore, 42 is also a factor of *a*.

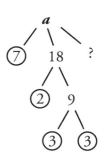

2. **CANNOT BE DETERMINED:**

If *r* is divisible by 80, its prime factors include 2, 2, 2, 2, and 5, as indicated by the factor tree to the right. Therefore, any integer that can be constructed as a product of any of these prime factors is also a factor of *r*. $15 = 3 \times 5$. Since the prime factor 3 is not in the factor tree, we cannot determine whether 15 is a factor of *r*. As numerical examples, we could take $r = 80$, in which case 15 is NOT a factor of *r*, or $r = 240$, in which case 15 IS a factor of *r*.

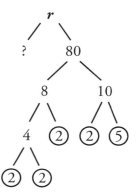

3. **YES:** If 2 numbers are both multiples of the same number, then their SUM is also a multiple of that same number. Since *n* and *p* share the common factor 7, the sum of *n* and *p* must also be divisible by 7.

4. **CANNOT BE DETERMINED:**

In order for 8 to be a factor of 2*g*, we would need two more 2's in the factor tree. By the Factor Foundation Rule, *g* would need to be divisible by 4. We know that *g* is not divisible by 8, but there are certainly integers that are divisible by 4 and not by 8, such as 4, 12, 20, 28, etc. However, while we cannot conclude that *g* is **not** divisible by 4, we cannot be certain that *g* **is** divisible by 4, either. As numerical examples, we could take $g = 5$, in which case 8 is NOT a factor of 2*g*, or $g = 4$, in which case 8 IS a factor of 2*g*.

5. **CANNOT BE DETERMINED:**

If *j* is divisible by 12 and by 10, its prime factors include 2, 2, 3, and 5, as indicated by the factor tree to the left. There are only TWO 2's that are definitely in the prime factorization of *j*, because the 2 in the prime factorization of 10 may be REDUNDANT—that is, it may be the SAME 2 as one of the 2's in the prime factorization of 12.

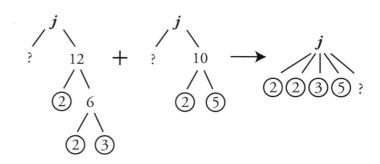

$24 = 2 \times 2 \times 2 \times 3$. There are only two 2's in the prime box of *j*; 24 requires three 2's. Therefore, 24 is not necessarily a factor of *j*.

As another way to prove that we cannot determine whether 24 is a factor of *j*, consider 60. The number 60 is divisible by both 12 and 10. However, it is NOT divisible by 24. Therefore, *j* could equal 60, in which case it is not divisible by 24. Alternatively, *j* could equal 120, in which case it IS divisible by 24.

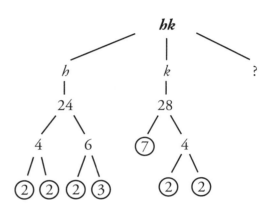

6. CANNOT BE DETERMINED:

If *xyz* is divisible by 12, its prime factors include 2, 2, and 3, as indicated by the factor tree to the right. Those prime factors could all be factors of *x* and *y*, in which case 12 is a factor of *xy*. For example, this is the case when *x* = 20, *y* = 3, and *z* = 7. However, *x* and *y* could be prime or otherwise not divisible by 2, 2, and 3, in which case *xy* is not divisible by 12. For example, this is the case when *x* = 5, *y* = 11, and *z* = 24.

7. YES: By the Factor Foundation Rule, if 6 is a factor of *r* and *r* is a factor of *s*, then 6 is a factor of *s*.

8. YES:

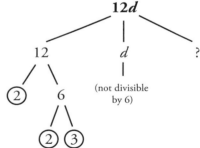

By the Factor Foundation Rule, all the factors of both *h* and *k* must be factors of the product, *hk*. Therefore, the factors of *hk* include 2, 2, 2, 2, 2, 3, and 7, as shown in the combined factor tree to the right. 21 = 3 × 7. Both 3 and 7 are in the tree. Therefore, 21 is a factor of *hk*.

9. YES:

The fact that *d* is not divisible by 6 is irrelevant in this case. Since 12 is divisible by 6, 12*d* is also divisible by 6.

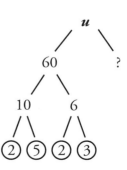

10. CANNOT BE DETERMINED:

If *u* is divisible by 60, its prime factors include 2, 2, 3, and 5, as indicated by the factor tree to the right. Therefore, any integer that can be constructed as a product of any of these prime factors is also a factor of *u*. 18 = 2 × 3 × 3. Since there is only one 3 in the factor tree, we cannot determine whether or not 18 is a factor of *u*. As numerical examples, we could take *u* = 60, in which case 18 is NOT a factor of *u*, or *u* = 180, in which case 18 IS a factor of *u*.

11. **C:** The prime factorization of 40 is $2 \times 2 \times 2 \times 5$. 40 has 2 distinct prime factors: 2 and 5. The prime factorization of 50 is $5 \times 5 \times 2$. 50 also has two distinct prime factors: 2 and 5. Therefore, the **two quantities are equal.**

12. **B:** Simplify Quantity A first. There is only one even prime number: 2. Therefore Quantity A is $12 \times 2 = 24$.

Quantity A	**Quantity B**
The product of 12 and an even prime number =	The sum of the greatest four factors of 12
$12 \times 2 = 24$	$12 + 6 + 4 + 3 = 25$

The four greatest factors of 12 are 12, 6, 4 and 3. $12 + 6 + 4 + 3 = 25$. Therefore, **Quantity B is greater.**

13. **C:** When 20 is divided by 12, the result is a quotient of 1 and a remainder of 8 ($12 \times 1 + 8 = 20$).

When 32 is divided by 12, the result is a quotient of 2 and a remainder of 8 ($12 \times 2 + 8 = 32$).

$$x = 20, y = 32 \text{ and } z = 12$$

Quantity A	**Quantity B**
8	8

Therefore, the **two quantities are equal.**

14. **9:** Since $\dfrac{a}{b}$ has a remainder of 4, b must be at least 5 (remember, the remainder must *always* be smaller than the divisor). The smallest possible value for a is 4 (it could also be 9, 14, 19, etc.) Thus, the smallest possible value for $a + b$ is 9.

15. **0:** Because $\dfrac{x}{y}$ has a remainder of 0, x is divisible by y. Therefore xz will be divisible by y, and so will have a remainder of 0 when divided by y.

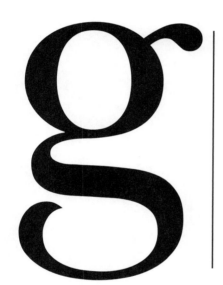

Chapter 3
of
NUMBER PROPERTIES

ODDS & EVENS

In This Chapter . . .

- Arithmetic Rules of Odds & Evens
- The Sum of Two Primes
- Testing Odd & Even Cases

ODDS & EVENS

Even numbers are integers that are divisible by 2. Odd numbers are integers that are not divisible by 2. All integers are either even or odd.

Evens: 0, 2, 4, 6, 8, 10, 12…   Odds: 1, 3, 5, 7, 9, 11…

Consecutive integers alternate between even and odd: 9, 10, 11, 12, 13…
                                                            O, E, O, E, O…

Negative integers are also either even or odd:

Evens: −2, −4, −6, −8, −10, −12…   Odds: −1, −3, −5, −7, −9, −11…

Arithmetic Rules of Odds & Evens

The GRE tests your knowledge of how odd and even numbers combine through addition, subtraction, multiplication, and division. Rules for adding, subtracting, multiplying and dividing odd and even numbers can be derived by simply picking numbers and testing them out. While this is certainly a valid strategy, it also pays to memorize the following rules for operating with odds and evens, as they are extremely useful for certain GRE math questions.

Addition and Subtraction:
Add or subtract 2 odds or 2 evens, and the result is EVEN. $7 + 11 = 18$ and $14 − 6 = 8$
Add or subtract an odd with an even, and the result is ODD. $7 + 8 = 15$

Multiplication:
When you multiply integers, if ANY of the integers are $3 \times \mathbf{8} \times 9 \times 13 = 2,808$
even, the result is EVEN.

Likewise, if NONE of the integers are even, then the result is ODD. $3 \times 5 \times 7 = 105$

If you multiply together several even integers, the result will be divisible by higher and higher powers of 2. This result should make sense from our discussion of prime factors. Each even number will contribute at least one 2 to the factors of the product.

For example, if there are TWO even integers in a set of integers being multipled together, the result will be divisible by 4. $\mathbf{2} \times 5 \times \mathbf{6} = 60$ (divisible by 4)

If there are THREE even integers in a set of integers being multipled together, the result will be divisible by 8.
          $\mathbf{2} \times 5 \times \mathbf{6} \times \mathbf{10} = 600$ (divisible by 8)

To summarize so far:

      Odd $\pm$ Even = ODD   Odd $\times$ Odd = ODD
      Odd $\pm$ Odd = EVEN   Even $\times$ Even = EVEN (and divisible by 4)
      Even $\pm$ Even = EVEN   Odd $\times$ Even = EVEN

Division:

There are no guaranteed outcomes in division, because the division of two integers may not yield an integer result. There are several potential outcomes, depending upon the value of the dividend and divisor.

Divisibility of Odds & Evens

	Even?	**Odd?**	**Non-Integer?**
Even ÷ Even	✓ Example: $12 \div 2 = 6$	✓ Example: $12 \div 4 = 3$	✓ Example: $12 \div 8 = 1.5$
Even ÷ Odd	✓ Example: $12 \div 3 = 4$	✗	✓ Example: $12 \div 5 = 2.4$
Odd ÷ Even	✗	✗	✓ Example: $9 \div 6 = 1.5$
Odd ÷ Odd	✗	✓ Example: $15 \div 5 = 3$	✓ Example: $15 \div 25 = 0.6$

An odd number divided by any other integer CANNOT produce an even integer. Also, an odd number divided by an even number CANNOT produce an integer, because the odd number will never be divisible by the factor of 2 concealed within the even number.

Check Your Skills

For 1–3, say whether the expression will be odd or even.

1. $1{,}007{,}425 \times 305{,}313 + 2$
2. $5 \times 778 \times 3 \times 4 + 1$
3. The sum of four consecutive integers.
4. Will the product of two odd integers divided by a multiple of two be an integer?

Answers can be found on page 63.

The Sum of Two Primes

Notice that all prime numbers are odd, except the number 2. (All larger even numbers are divisible by 2, so they cannot be prime.) Thus, the sum of any two primes will be even ("Add two odds..."), unless one of those primes is the number 2. So, if you see a sum of two primes that is odd, one of those primes must be the number 2. Conversely, if you know that 2 CANNOT be one of the primes in the sum, then the sum of the two primes must be even.

> If *a* and *b* are both prime numbers greater than 10, which of the following *must* be true?
> Indicate *all* that apply.
>
> [A] *b* is an even number.
> [B] The difference between *a* and *b* equals 117.
> [C] The sum of *a* and *b* is even.

Since *a* and *b* are both prime numbers greater than 10, they must both be odd. Therefore *ab* must be an odd number, so Choice A cannot be true. Similarly, if *a* and *b* are both odd, then $a - b$ cannot equal 117 (an odd number). This difference must be even. Therefore, Choice B cannot be true. Finally, since *a* and *b* are both odd, $a + b$ must be even, so Choice C will always be true.

Check Your Skills

5. The difference between the factors of prime number *x* is one. The difference between the factors of prime number *y* is two. Is *xy* even?

Answers can be found on page 63.

Testing Odd & Even Cases

Sometimes multiple variables can be odd or even, and you need to determine the implications of each possible scenario. In that case, set up a table listing all the possible odd/even combinations of the variables, and determine what effect that would have on the question.

> If *a*, *b*, and *c* are integers and $ab + c$ is odd, which of the following *must* be true?
> Indicate *all* that apply.
>
> [A] $a + c$ is odd
> [B] $b + c$ is odd
> [C] abc is even

Here, *a*, *b* and *c* could all possibly be odd or even. Some combinations of Odds & Evens for *a*, *b* and *c* will lead to an odd result. Other combinations will lead to an even result. We need to test each possible combination to see what the result will be for each. Set up a table, as shown below, and fill in the possibilities.

Scenario	a	b	c	$ab + c$
1	ODD	ODD	ODD	$O \times O + O = E$
2	**ODD**	**ODD**	**EVEN**	$O \times O + E = O$
3	**ODD**	**EVEN**	**ODD**	$O \times E + O = O$
4	ODD	EVEN	EVEN	$O \times E + E = E$
5	**EVEN**	**ODD**	**ODD**	$E \times O + O = O$
6	EVEN	ODD	EVEN	$E \times O + E = E$
7	**EVEN**	**EVEN**	**ODD**	$E \times E + O = O$
8	EVEN	EVEN	EVEN	$E \times E + E = E$

Scenarios 2, 3, 5 and 7 yield an odd result, and so we must focus only on those scenarios. We can conclude that Choice A need not be true (Scenario 3 yields $a + c =$ EVEN), Choice B need not be true (Scenario 5 yields $b + c =$ EVEN), and Choice C must be true (all 4 working scenarios yield $abc =$ EVEN). Therefore, the only correct answer is Choice C.

Check Your Skills

6. If $\dfrac{x}{y}$ is even, which of the following could be true?

   Indicate _all_ that apply.

   - [A] xy is odd
   - [B] xy is even
   - [C] $x + y$ is odd

7. If xyz is even, $x + z$ is odd, and $y + z$ is odd, z is:

   Choose just _one_ answer.

   (A) Even
   (B) Odd
   (C) Indeterminable (could be even or odd, or a fraction)

   Answers can be found on page 63–64.

Check Your Skills Answers

1. **Odd:** We have an odd multiplied by an odd, which always results in an odd. Then we add an even to the odd, which also results in an odd.

2. **Odd:** At least one of the numbers multiplied together is even, meaning the product will be even. When we add an odd to that even, we get an odd.

3. **Even:** Because integers go back and forth between evens and odds, the sum of any four consecutive integers can be expressed as Even + Even + Odd + Odd. Taking these one by one, we start with Even + Even = Even. Then we add an Odd to that Even, resulting in an Odd. Finally, we add another Odd to that Odd, resulting in an Even.

4. **No:** The product of two odd integers is always odd. Any multiple of two is even, and as the chart showed, an odd divided by an even cannot be an integer.

5. **Yes:** Prime numbers only have two factors: one and themselves. So if the difference between the factors of a prime number is one, its factors must be one and two. This means $x = 2$. By the same logic, y must be equal to 3 ($3 - 1 = 2$). The product of 2 and 3 is 6, so xy is even.

6. **B and C:** If x/y is even, then either x and y are both even, or x is even and y is odd. Let's make a chart:

Scenario	x	y	x/y	xy	$x + y$
1	E	E	**Even or Odd or Non-int.**	**Even**	**Even**
2	E	O	**Even or Non-int.**	**Even**	**Odd**
3	O	E	Non-int.	Even	Odd
4	O	O	Odd or Non-int.	Odd	Even

The question stem stipulates that x/y is even. This is only possible in the first two scenarios. In both of those situations, xy is even. This means that Choice A is untrue, but Choice B is true. While $x + y$ can be either even or odd, that means that it *could* be odd, so Choice C also works.

7. **C:** Indeterminable. Once again, let's make a chart.

As we can see, there are two rows where xyz is even, $x + z$ is odd, and $y + z$ is odd. z is even in one case and odd in another.

Scenario	x	y	z	xyz	$x + z$	$y + z$
1	E	E	E	E	E	E
2	**E**	**E**	**O**	**E**	**O**	**O**
3	E	O	E	E	E	O
4	E	O	O	E	O	E
5	O	E	E	E	O	E
6	O	E	O	E	E	O
7	**O**	**O**	**E**	**E**	**O**	**O**
8	O	O	O	O	E	E

Problem Set

For questions #1–15, answer each question ODD, EVEN, or CANNOT BE DETERMINED. Try to explain each answer using the rules you learned in this section. All variables in problems #1–15 are assumed to be integers unless otherwise indicated.

1. If n is odd, p is even, and q is odd, what is $n + p + q$?

2. If r is a prime number greater than 2, and s is odd, what is rs?

3. If t is odd, what is t^4?

4. If u is even and w is odd, what is $u + uw$?

5. If $x \div y$ yields an odd integer, what is x?

6. If $a + b$ is even, what is ab?

7. If c, d, and e are consecutive integers, what is cde?

8. If f and g are prime numbers, what is $f + g$?

9. If h is even, j is odd, and k is odd, what is $k(h + j)$?

10. If m is odd, what is $m^2 + m$?

11. If n, p, q, and r are consecutive integers, what is their sum?

12. If $t = s - 3$, what is $s + t$?

13. If u is odd and w is even, what is $(uw)^2 + u$?

14. If xy is even and z is even, what is $x + z$?

15. If a, b, and c are consecutive integers, what is $a + b + c$?

16.

> 202 divided by some prime number x yields an odd number. 411 multiplied by some prime number y yields an even number.

Quantity A	**Quantity B**
x	y

17.

Quantity A	**Quantity B**
The tenths digit of the product of two even integers divided by 4	The tenths digit of the product of an even and an odd integer divided by 4

18.

x is a non-negative even integer

Quantity A	**Quantity B**
x	1

1. **EVEN:** O + E = O. O + O = E. If in doubt, try plugging in actual numbers: 7 + 2 + 3 = 12 (even).

2. **ODD:** O × O = O. If in doubt, try plugging in actual numbers: 3 × 5 = 15 (odd).

3. **ODD:** O × O × O × O = O. If in doubt, try plugging in actual numbers: 3 × 3 × 3 × 3 = 81 (odd).

4. **EVEN:** *uw* is even. Therefore, E + E = E.

5. **CANNOT BE DETERMINED:** There are no guaranteed outcomes in division.

6. **CANNOT BE DETERMINED:** If $a + b$ is even, a and b are either both odd or both even. If they are both odd, ab is odd. If they are both even, ab is even.

7. **EVEN:** At least one of the consecutive integers, c, d, and e, must be even. Therefore, the product cde must be even.

8. **CANNOT BE DETERMINED:** If either f or g is 2, then $f + g$ will be odd. If f and g are odd primes, or if f and g are both 2, then $f + g$ will be even.

9. **ODD:** $h + j$ must be odd (E + O = O). Therefore, $k(h + j)$ must be odd (O × O = O).

10. **EVEN:** m^2 must be odd (O × O = O). $m^2 + m$, therefore, must be even (O + O = E).

11. **EVEN:** If n, p, q, and r are consecutive integers, two of them must be odd and two of them must be even. You can pair them up to add them: O + O = E, and E + E = E. Adding the pairs, you will see that the sum must be even: E + E = E.

12. **ODD:** If s is even, then t must be odd. If s is odd, then t must be even. Either way, the sum must be odd: E + O = O, or O + E = O.

13. **ODD:** $(uw)^2$ must be even. Therefore, E + O = O.

14. **CANNOT BE DETERMINED:** If xy is even, then either x or y (or both x and y) must be even. Given that z is even, $x + z$ could be O + E or E + E. Therefore, we cannot determine whether $x + z$ is odd or even.

15. **CANNOT BE DETERMINED:** If a, b, and c are consecutive, then there could be either one or two even integers in the set. $a + b + c$ could be O + E + O or E + O + E. In the first case, the sum is even; in the second, the sum is odd.

16. **C:** An even divided by an odd can never yield an odd quotient. This means the prime number x must be even (because otherwise you'd have 202/odd, which wouldn't yield an odd quotient). The only even prime number is 2, so x = 2. Similarly, an odd times an odd will always be odd, so y must be even. The only prime even number is 2, so y = 2.

Quantity A	**Quantity B**
$\dfrac{202}{x} = \text{odd} \rightarrow \dfrac{202}{2} = 101$	$411 \times y = \text{even} \rightarrow 411 \times 2 = 822$
$x = 2$	$y = 2$

17. **D:** This question could be solved either by trying out numbers or making a chart. For Quantity A, the product of two even integers will always divide evenly by 4 because each even number has a 2 in its prime tree. For instance, $2 \times 2 = 4$, $2 \times 4 = 8$, $2 \times 6 = 12$. All of these numbers are divisible by 4. The tenths digit will always have a zero in it (ie. 4.*0*, 8.*0*, 12.*0*).

The tenths digit of the product of an even and an odd integer *could* be divisible by 4. For example, $4 \times 5 = 20$, and $\dfrac{20}{4} = 5$, the tenths digit of which is 0. However, it could also *not* be divisible by 4. For example, $2 \times 5 = 10$, and $\dfrac{10}{4} = 2.5$, the tenths digit of which is 5. Because the two quantities could be equal or different, the answer must be Choice D. **We do not have enough information** to determine which quantity is greater.

18. **D:** Always be careful when dealing with evens and odds. While 0 is neither positive nor negative, it *is* even. Thus, the first possible value of x here is 0, not 2. Thus x could be either less than or greater than 1. **We do not have enough information** to determine which quantity is greater.

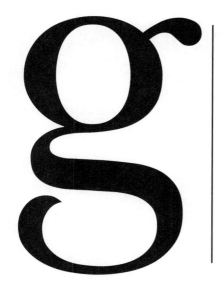

Chapter 4
of
NUMBER PROPERTIES

POSITIVES & NEGATIVES

In This Chapter . . .

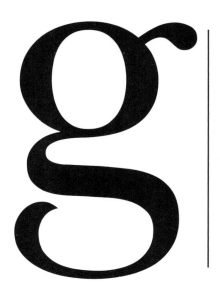

- Absolute Value: Absolutely Positive
- A Double Negative = A Positive
- Multiplying & Dividing Signed Numbers
- Testing Positive & Negative Cases

POSITIVES & NEGATIVES

Numbers can be either positive or negative (except the number 0, which is neither). A number line illustrates this idea:

Negative numbers are all to the left of zero. Positive numbers are all to the right of zero.

Note that a variable (such as x) can have either a positive or a negative value, unless there is evidence otherwise. The variable x is not necessarily positive, nor is $-x$ necessarily negative.

Absolute Value: Absolutely Positive

The absolute value of a number answers this question: **How far away is the number from 0 on the number line?** For example, the number 5 is exactly 5 units away from 0, so the absolute value of 5 equals 5. Mathematically, we write this using the symbol for absolute value: $|5| = 5$. To find the absolute value of -5, look at the number line above: -5 is also exactly 5 units away from 0. Thus, the absolute value of -5 equals 5, or, in mathematical symbols, $|-5| = 5$. Notice that absolute value is always positive, because it disregards the direction (positive or negative) from which the number approaches 0 on the number line. When you interpret a number in an absolute value sign, just think: Absolutely Positive! (Except, of course, for 0, because $|0| = 0$, which is the smallest possible absolute value.)

On the number line above, note that 5 and -5 are the same distance from 0, which is located halfway between them. In general, if two numbers are opposites of each other, then they have the same absolute value, and 0 is halfway between. If $x = -y$, then we have either

(We cannot tell which variable is positive without more information.)

A Double Negative = A Positive

A double negative occurs when a minus sign is in front of a negative number (which already has its own negative sign). For example:

> What is $7 - (-3)$?

Just as you learned in English class, two negatives yield a positive:

> $7 - (-3) = 7 + 3 = 10$.

This is a very easy step to miss, especially when the double negative is somewhat hidden.

> What is $7 - (12 - 9)$?

Many people will make the mistake of computing this as $7 - 12 - 9 = -14$. However, notice that the second term in the expression in parentheses has a double negative. Therefore, this expression should be calculated as $7 - 12 + 9 = 4$.

Check Your Skills

1. Does $|-5| + |5| + |-5| = |15|$?

2. If $4y - (x - 4) = 4x + (-y + 4)$, and neither x nor $y = 0$, what is $\dfrac{x}{y}$?

Answers can be found on page 75.

Multiplying & Dividing Signed Numbers

When you multiply or divide two numbers, positive or negative, follow one simple rule:

If **S**igns are the **S**ame, the answer's po**S**itive
but if **N**ot, the answer is **N**egative.

$7 \times 8 = 56$ & $(-7) \times (-8) = 56$
$(-7) \times 8 = -56$ & $7 \times (-8) = -56$

$56 \div 7 = 8$ & $-56 \div (-8) = 7$
$56 \div (-7) = -8$ & $-56 \div 8 = -7$

That is, a positive × a positive or a negative × a negative will result in a positive. A positive times a negative will result in a negative.

This principle can be extended to multiplication and division by more than two numbers. For example, if 3 numbers are multiplied together, the result will be positive if there are NO negative numbers, or TWO negative numbers. The result will be negative if there is ONE or THREE negative numbers.

We can summarize this pattern as follows. When you multiply or divide a group of nonzero numbers, the result will be positive if you have an EVEN number of negative numbers. The result will be negative if you have an ODD number of negative numbers.

Check Your Skills

3. Is the product $-12 \times -15 \times 3 \times 4 \times 5 \times -2$ positive or negative?
4. If $xy \neq 0$, is $-x \times -y$ definitely positive?

Answers can be found on page 75.

Testing Positive & Negative Cases

Some Positives & Negatives problems deal with multiple variables, each of which can be positive or negative. In these situations, you should set up a table listing all the possible positive/negative combinations of the variables, and determine what effect that would have on the question. For example:

If $ab > 0$, which of the following must be negative?

(A) $a + b$ (B) $|a| + b$ (C) $b - a$ (D) $\dfrac{a}{b}$ (E) $-\dfrac{a}{b}$

One way to solve problems such as this one is to test numbers systematically. In this example, we can test each of the four possible positive/negative combinations of a and b to see whether they meet the criteria established in the question. Then we eliminate any that do not meet these criteria. Finally, we test each of the remaining combinations in each of the answer choices. You can use a chart such as the one below to keep track of your work, choosing simple values (e.g. 3 and 6) to make calculations quickly:

	Criterion: $ab > 0$	A $a + b$	B $\lvert a \rvert + b$	C $b - a$	D $\dfrac{a}{b}$	E $-\dfrac{a}{b}$
+, + $a = 3$ $b = 6$	YES	POS	POS	POS	POS	NEG
−, + $a = -3$ $b = 6$	NO					
−, − $a = -3$ $b = -6$	YES	NEG	NEG	NEG	POS	NEG
+, − $a = 3$ $b = -6$	NO					

Notice that if more than one answer choice gives you the desired result for all cases, you can try another pair of numbers and test those answer choices again.

Another approach to this problem is to determine what you know from the fact that $ab > 0$. If $ab > 0$, then the signs of a and b must both be the same (both positive or both negative). This should lead you to answer choice (E), since $-\dfrac{a}{b}$ must be negative if a and b have the same sign.

Check Your Skills

5. The absolute value of x is greater than the absolute value of y. Which of the following must be true? Indicate _all_ that apply.

   A xy is positive
   B $x + y > 0$
   C $x^2 > y^2$

6. If $ab < 0$, $a > b$, and $a > -b$, which of the following must be true?

   (A) $a/b > 0$
   (B) $a + b < 0$
   (C) $b - (-a) > 0$
   (D) $a/b = 1$
   (E) $a - b < 0$

Answers can be found on page 75–76.

Check Your Skills Answers

1. **Yes:** The absolute values of 5 and −5 are both 5, and $3 \times 5 = 15$.

2. **1:** This question is easy as long as you pay close attention to the signs. The left side of the equation will have a double negative (in front of the 4), so it simplifies to $4y − x + 4$. The right side has no double negative (in fact, the parentheses are a bit of a red herring), so it simplifies to $4x − y + 4$.

Our equation now reads:

$4y − x + 4 = 4x − y + 4$. Continue to simplify. $5y = 5x$, or $x = y$. If x and y are equal, then $\dfrac{x}{y} = 1$.

3. **Negative:** Here we see three negative numbers and three positive numbers. Two of the negative numbers will cancel each other out, and the third one will make the final product negative.

4. **No:** Always be careful when dealing with variables. Even though these two terms have negative signs in front of them, they aren't necessarily negative. This is because x or y could themselves be negative. If x and y are both positive or both negative, then they will both flip the other way with the negative sign, meaning they will still both be either positive or negative, in which case their product will be positive. But if x is positive and y is negative, then when we flip them, we will still end up with one positive and one negative, so the product will be negative.

5. **C:** What's more fun than making a chart? Nothing. Let's try looking at the four possible situations with x and y that maintain the requirement that the absolute value of x is greater than the absolute value of y.

Scenario	x	y	xy	$x + y$	x^2	y^2
1	5	3	15	8	25	9
2	−5	3	−15	−2	25	9
3	5	−3	−15	2	25	9
4	−5	−3	15	−8	25	9

The second scenario here gets rid of both Choice A and Choice B, because xy and $x + y$ are both negative. However, in every case, $x^2 > y^2$, so Choice C alone is necessarily true. You could also solve this by looking at each statement and keeping in mind what you know if the absolute value of x is greater than the absolute value of y. You don't know if xy is positive because x or y could be negative.

6. **C:** Though a bit tricky, the given information here tells you everything you need to know about a and b. Instead of testing numbers to get through the answer choices (as above), we can test numbers to make sense of the given information. First, if $ab < 0$, then the two variables must have opposite signs. Second, if $a > b$, then a must be the positive number, and b the negative number. Finally, if $a > −b$, a must have a larger absolute value than b (if $a = 4$ and $b = −5$, then $−b > a$, which is the opposite of what we want).

Now, it should be enough just to walk through the answer choices.

A) $\dfrac{a}{b} > 0$

   UNTRUE. If a and b have opposite signs, then the quotient will be negative (as per our rules).

B) $a + b < 0$

   UNTRUE. We know that a is positive and has a larger absolute value than b. No matter what a and b are, their sum has to be positive.

C) $b - (-a) > 0$

   TRUE. This actually simplifies to look like the equation in answer choice B, though with the sign switched. We already know this has to be true.

D) $\dfrac{a}{b} = 1$.

   UNTRUE. The quotient of a positive and a negative number must be negative, so can never be 1.

E) $a - b < 0$

   UNTRUE. If you subtract a negative number from a positive number, you'll be left with an even bigger positive number.

Problem Set

Solve problems #1–5. <u>Don't use the calculator.</u>

1.   Evaluate $2|x - y| + |z + w|$ if $x = 2$, $y = 5$, $z = -3$, and $w = 8$.

2.   Simplify $66 \div (-33) \times |-9|$

3.   Simplify $\dfrac{-30}{5} - \dfrac{18 - 9}{-3}$

4.   Simplify $\dfrac{20 \times (-7)}{-35 \times (-2)}$

5.   When is $|x - 4|$ equal to $4 - x$?

In problems #6–15, decide whether the expression described is POSITIVE, NEGATIVE, or CANNOT BE DETERMINED. If you answer CANNOT BE DETERMINED, give numerical examples to show how the problem could be either positive or negative.

6.   The product of 3 negative numbers

7.   The quotient of one negative and one positive number

8. xy, given that $x < 0$ and $y \neq 0$

9. $|x| \times y^2$, given that $xy \neq 0$

10. $\dfrac{x}{y} \div z$, given that x, y, and z are negative

11. $\dfrac{|ab|}{b}$, given that $b < a < 0$

12. $-4|d|$, given that $d \neq 0$

13. $\dfrac{rst}{w}$, given that $r < s < 0 < w < t$

14. $h^4k^3m^2$, given that $k < 0$ and $hm \neq 0$

15. $\dfrac{-x}{(-y)(-z)}$, given that $xyz > 0$

16.

$$xy > 0$$

Quantity A	**Quantity B**
$\dfrac{x}{|x|}$	$\dfrac{y}{|y|}$

17.

Quantity A	**Quantity B**
$-a \times -a \times a \times a$	-1

18.

$$|x| = |y|, x \neq 0$$

Quantity A	**Quantity B**
$x + y$	$2x$

1. **11:** $2|x - y| + |z + w| = 2|2 - 5| + |-3 + 8| = 2|-3| + |5| = 2(3) + 5 = 11$. Note that when you deal with more complicated absolute value expressions, such as $|x - y|$ in this example, you should NEVER change individual signs to "+" signs! For instance, in this problem $|x - y| = |2 - 5|$, not $|2 + 5|$.

2 **−18:** In division, use the Same Sign rule. In this case, the signs are not the same. Therefore, $66 \div (-33)$ yields a negative number (-2). Then, multiply by the absolute value of -9, which is 9. To multiply -2×9, use the Same Sign rule: the signs are not the same, so the answer is negative. Remember to apply division and multiplication from left to right: first the division, then the multiplication.

3. **−3:** This is a two-step subtraction problem. Use the Same Sign rule for both steps. In the first step, the signs are different; therefore, the answer is negative. In the second step, the signs are again different. That result is negative. The final answer is $-6 - (-3) = -3$.

4. **−2:** The sign of the first product, $20 \times (-7)$, is negative (by the Same Sign rule). The sign of the second product, $-35 \times (-2)$, is positive (by the Same Sign rule). Applying the Same Sign rule to the final division problem, the final answer must be negative.

5. $x \le 4$: Absolute value brackets can only do one of two things to the expression inside of them: (a) leave the expression unchanged, whenever the expression is 0 or positive, or (b) change the sign of the whole expression, whenever the expression is 0 or negative. (Notice that both outcomes occur when the expression is zero, because "negative 0" and "positive 0" are equal.) In this case, the sign of the whole expression $x - 4$ is being changed, resulting in $-(x - 4) = 4 - x$. This will happen only if the expression $x - 4$ is 0 or negative. Therefore $x - 4 \le 0$, or $x \le 4$.

6. **NEGATIVE:** The product of the first two negative numbers is positive. A positive times a negative is negative.

7. **NEGATIVE:** By the Same Sign rule, the quotient of a negative and a positive number must be negative.

8. **CANNOT BE DETERMINED:** x is negative. However, y could be either positive or negative. Therefore, we have no way to determine whether the product xy is positive or negative.

9. **POSITIVE:** $|x|$ is positive because absolute value can never be negative, and $x \ne 0$ (since $xy \ne 0$). Also, y^2 is positive because y^2 will be either positive × positive or negative × negative (and $y \ne 0$). The product of two positive numbers is positive, by the Same Sign rule.

10. **NEGATIVE:** Do this problem in two steps: First, a negative number divided by a negative number yields a positive number (by the Same Sign rule). Second, a positive number divided by a negative number yields a negative number (again, by the Same Sign rule).

11. **NEGATIVE:** a and b are both negative. Therefore, this problem is a positive number (by the definition of absolute value) divided by a negative number. By the Same Sign rule, the answer will be negative.

12. **NEGATIVE:** You do not need to know the sign of d to solve this problem. Because d is within the absolute value symbols, you can treat the expression $|d|$ as a positive number (since we know that $d \ne 0$). By the Same Sign rule, a negative number times a positive number yields a negative number.

13. **POSITIVE:** r and s are negative; w and t are positive. Therefore, rst is a positive number. A positive number divided by another positive number yields a positive number.

14. **NEGATIVE:** Nonzero numbers raised to even exponents always yield positive numbers. Therefore, h^4 and m^2 are both positive. Because k is negative, k^3 is negative. Therefore, the final product, $h^4k^3m^2$, is the product of two positives and a negative, which is negative.

15. **NEGATIVE:** Simplifying the original fraction yields: $\dfrac{-x}{yz}$.

If the product xyz is positive, then there are two possible scenarios: (1) all the integers are positive, or (2) two of the integers are negative and the third is positive. Test out both scenarios, using real numbers. In the first case, the end result is negative. In the second case, the two negative integers will essentially cancel each other out. Again, the end result is negative.

16. **C:** If $xy > 0$, x and y have the same sign. We already know that the denominator of both fractions described in the quantities will be positive. The numerator will either be positive for both, or negative for both. If both x and y are positive, the quantities simplify like this:

$$xy > 0$$

Quantity A	**Quantity B**
$\dfrac{x}{|x|} \to \dfrac{\text{positive } x}{\text{positive } x} \to 1$	$\dfrac{y}{|y|} \to \dfrac{\text{positive } y}{\text{positive } y} \to 1$

In this case, both quantities equal 1. If x and y are both negative, the quantities simplify like this:

$$xy > 0$$

Quantity A	**Quantity B**
$\dfrac{x}{|x|} \to \dfrac{\text{negative } x}{\text{positive } x} \to -1$	$\dfrac{y}{|y|} \to \dfrac{\text{negative } y}{\text{positive } y} \to -1$

In this case, both quantities equal −1. Either way, the values in the **two quantities are equal.**

17. **A:** If a is positive, then $-a$ is negative, and Quantity A can be rewritten as (negative) × (negative) × (positive) × (positive), which will result in a positive product.

If a is negative, then $-a$ is positive, and Quantity A can be rewritten as (positive) × (positive) × (negative) × (negative), which will result in a positive product.

In either of these situations, the quantities look like this:

Quantity A	**Quantity B**
positive	−1

Quantity A will be bigger.

The other possibility is that a is 0. If a is 0, then Quantity A looks like this:

Quantity A   **Quantity B**

$0 \times 0 \times 0 \times 0 = 0$ -1

Quantity A is therefore larger in either scenario.

18. **D:** If $|x| = |y|$, then the two numbers could either be equal (positive or negative), or opposite (one positive and one negative). The following chart shows all the possible arrangements if $|x| = |y| = 3$

x	y
3	3
3	-3
-3	3
-3	-3

If x and y are the same sign, then $x = y$. Substitute x for y in Quantity A.

$$|x| = |y|,\ x \neq 0$$

Quantity A   **Quantity B**

$x + (x) = 2x$ $2x$

If x and y are the same sign, the quantities are equal.

If x and y have opposite signs, then $-x = y$. Substitute $-x$ for y in Quantity A.

$$|x| = |y|,\ x \neq 0$$

Quantity A   **Quantity B**

$x + (-x) = 0$ $2x$

If x does not equal 0, then the values in the two quantities will be different. The correct answer is D—**we do not have enough information** to determine which quantity is greater.

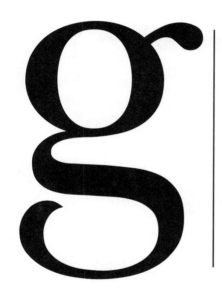

Chapter 5
of
NUMBER PROPERTIES

EXPONENTS

In This Chapter . . .

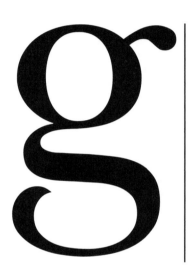

EXPONENTS

The mathematical expression 4^3 consists of a base (4) and an exponent (3).

The expression is read as "four to the third power." The base (4) is multiplied by itself as many times as the power requires (3).

Thus $4^3 = 4 \times 4 \times 4 = 64$.

Two exponents have special names: the exponent 2 is called the square, and the exponent 3 is called the cube.

5^2 can be read as five to the second power, or as five squared ($5^2 = 5 \times 5 = 25$).
5^3 can be read as five to the third power, or as five cubed ($5^3 = 5 \times 5 \times 5 = 125$).

Wow, That Increased Exponentially!

Have you ever heard the expression: "Wow, that increased exponentially!"? This phrase captures the essence of exponents. When a positive number greater than 1 increases exponentially, it does not merely increase; it increases a whole lot in a short amount of time.

An important property of exponents is that the greater the exponent, the faster the rate of increase. Consider the following progression:

$5^1 = 5$
$5^2 = 25$ Increased by 20
$5^3 = 125$ Increased by 100
$5^4 = 625$ Increased by 500

The important thing to remember is that, for positive bases bigger than 1, the greater the exponent, the faster the rate of increase.

All About the Base

THE SIGN OF THE BASE

The base of an exponential expression may be either positive or negative. With a negative base, simply multiply the negative number as many times as the exponent requires.

For example:

$$(-4)^2 = (-4) \times (-4) = 16 \qquad (-4)^3 = (-4) \times (-4) \times (-4) = -64$$

Consider this problem:

If $x^2 = 16$, is x equal to 4?

Your initial inclination is probably to say yes. However, x may not be 4; it may be -4. Thus, we cannot answer the question without additional information. We must be told that x is positive in order to affirm that x is 4. Beware whenever you see an even exponent on the test.

THE EVEN EXPONENT IS DANGEROUS: IT HIDES THE SIGN OF THE BASE!
One of the GRE's most common tricks involves the even exponent. In many cases, when an integer is raised to a power, the answer keeps the original sign of the base.

Examples:

$3^2 = 9$	$(-3)^3 = -27$	$3^3 = 27$
(positive base,	(negative base,	(positive base,
positive result)	negative result)	positive result)

However, any base raised to an even power will always result in a positive answer. This is because even if the underlying base is negative, there will be an EVEN number of negative signs in the product, and an even number of negative signs in a product makes the product positive.

Examples:

$3^2 = 9$	$(-3)^2 = 9$	$(-3)^4 = 81$
(positive base,	(negative base,	(negative base,
positive result)	positive result)	positive result)

Therefore, when a base is raised to an even exponent, the resulting answer may either keep or change the original sign of the base. Whether $x = 3$ or -3, $x^2 = 9$. This makes even exponents extremely dangerous, and the GRE loves to try to trick you with them.

Note that odd exponents are harmless, since they always keep the original sign of the base. For example, if you have the equation $x^3 = 64$, you can be sure that $x = 4$. You know that x is not -4 because $(-4)^3$ would yield -64.

Check Your Skills

1. $x \cdot x \cdot x = -27$, what is x?
2. $x^2 \cdot x^3 \cdot x = 64$, what is x?

Answers can be found on page 95.

A BASE OF 0, 1, or -1
   • An exponential expression with a base of 0 always yields 0, regardless of the exponent.
   • An exponential expression with a base of 1 always yields 1, regardless of the exponent.
   • An exponential expression with a base of -1 yields 1 when the exponent is even, and yields -1 when the exponent is odd.

For example, $0^3 = 0 \times 0 \times 0 = 0$ and $0^4 = 0 \times 0 \times 0 \times 0 = 0$.
Similarly, $1^3 = 1 \times 1 \times 1 = 1$ and $1^4 = 1 \times 1 \times 1 \times 1 = 1$.
Finally, $(-1)^3 = (-1) \times (-1) \times (-1) = -1$, but $(-1)^4 = (-1) \times (-1) \times (-1) \times (-1) = 1$.

Thus, if you are told that $x^6 = x^7 = x^{15}$, you know that x must be either 0 or 1. Do not try to do algebra on the equation. Simply plug 0 and 1 to check that the equation makes sense. Note that -1 does not fit the equation, since $(-1)^6 = 1$, but $(-1)^7 = -1$.

Of course, if you are told that $x^6 = x^8 = x^{10}$, x could be 0, 1 or −1. Any one of these three values fits the equation as given. (See why even exponents are so dangerous?)

Check Your Skills

3. $x^4 \cdot x^{-4} = y$, what is y?
4. $x^3 - x = 0$ and $x^2 + x^2 = 2$, what is x?

Answers can be found on page 95.

A FRACTIONAL BASE

When the base of an exponential expression is a positive proper fraction (in other words, a fraction between 0 and 1), an interesting thing occurs: as the exponent increases, the value of the expression decreases!

$$\left(\frac{3}{4}\right)^1 = \frac{3}{4} \qquad \left(\frac{3}{4}\right)^2 = \frac{3}{4} \times \frac{3}{4} = \frac{9}{16} \qquad \left(\frac{3}{4}\right)^3 = \frac{3}{4} \times \frac{3}{4} \times \frac{3}{4} = \frac{27}{64}$$

Notice that $\frac{3}{4} > \frac{9}{16} > \frac{27}{64}$. Increasing powers cause positive fractions to decrease.

We could also distribute the exponent before multiplying. For example:

$$\left(\frac{3}{4}\right)^1 = \frac{3^1}{4^1} = \frac{3}{4} \qquad \left(\frac{3}{4}\right)^2 = \frac{3^2}{4^2} = \frac{9}{16} \qquad \left(\frac{3}{4}\right)^2 = \frac{3^3}{4^3} = \frac{27}{64}$$

Note that, just like proper fractions, decimals between 0 and 1 decrease as their exponent increases:

$$(0.6)^2 = 0.36 \qquad\qquad (0.5)^4 = 0.0625 \qquad (0.1)^5 = 0.00001$$

Check Your Skills

5. Which is bigger, $\left(\frac{3}{4}\right)^2$ or $(0.8)^2$?

6. Which is bigger, $\frac{10}{7}$ or $\left(\frac{10}{7}\right)^2$?

Answers can be found on page 95.

A COMPOUND BASE

When the base of an exponential expression is a product, we can multiply the base together and then raise it to the exponent, OR we can distribute the exponent to each number in the base.

$$(2 \times 5)^3 = (10)^3 = 1,000 \qquad\qquad \textbf{OR} \qquad\qquad (2 \times 5)^3 = 2^3 \times 5^3 = 8 \times 125 = 1,000$$

You cannot do this with a sum, however. You must add the numbers inside the parentheses first.

$$(2 + 5)^3 = (7)^3 = 343 \qquad\qquad (2 + 5)^3 \neq 2^3 + 5^3$$

All About the Exponent

<u>THE SIGN OF THE EXPONENT</u>
An exponent is not always positive. What happens if the exponent is negative?

$$5^{-1} = \frac{1}{5^1} = \frac{1}{5} \qquad\qquad \frac{1}{4^{-2}} = \frac{1}{\frac{1}{4^2}} = 4^2 = 16 \qquad\qquad (-2)^{-3} = \frac{1}{(-2)^3} = -\frac{1}{8}$$

Very simply, negative exponents mean "put the term containing the exponent in the denominator of a fraction, and make the exponent positive." In other words, we divide by the base a certain number of times, rather than multiply. An expression with a negative exponent is the reciprocal of what that expression would be with a positive exponent. **When you see a negative exponent, think reciprocal!**

$$\left(\frac{3}{4}\right)^{-3} = \left(\frac{4}{3}\right)^3 = \frac{64}{27}$$

<u>AN EXPONENT OF 1</u>
Any base raised to the exponent of 1 keeps the original base. This is fairly intuitive.

$$3^1 = 3 \qquad\qquad 4^1 = 4 \qquad\qquad (-6)^1 = -6 \qquad\qquad \left(-\frac{1}{2}\right)^1 = -\frac{1}{2}$$

However, a fact that is not always obvious is that **any number that does not have an exponent implicitly has an exponent of 1**.

$$3 \times 3^4 = ?$$

In this case, just pretend that the "3" term has an exponent of 1 and proceed.

$$3^1 \times 3^4 = 3^{(1+4)} = 3^5 \qquad\qquad \text{Likewise, } 3 \times 3^x = 3^1 \times 3^x = 3^{(1+x)} = 3^{x+1}$$

Rule: When you see a base without an exponent, write in an exponent of 1.

<u>AN EXPONENT OF 0</u>
By definition, any nonzero base raised to the 0 power yields 1. This may not seem intuitive.

$$3^0 = 1 \qquad\qquad 4^0 = 1 \qquad\qquad (-6)^0 = 1 \qquad\qquad \left(-\frac{1}{2}\right)^0 = 1$$

To understand this fact, think of division of a number by itself, which is one way a zero exponent could occur.

$$\frac{3^7}{3^7} = 3^{(7-7)} = 3^0 = 1$$

When we divide 3^7 by itself, the result equals 1. Also, by applying the subtraction rule of exponents, we see that 3^7 divided by itself yields 3^0. Therefore, 3^0 MUST equal 1.

Note also that 0^0 is indeterminate and **never** appears on the GRE. Zero is the ONLY number that, when raised to the zero power, does not necessarily equal 1.

Rule: Any nonzero base raised to the power of zero (e.g. 3^0) is equal to 1.

Check Your Skills

7. $2 \cdot 2^x = 16$, what is x?

8. $\dfrac{5^{y+2}}{5^3} = 1$, what is y?

9. $\left(\dfrac{1}{2}\right)^y = \dfrac{1}{4} \times 2^y$, what is y?

Answers can be found on page 95.

Combining Exponential Terms

Imagine that we have a string of five a's (all multiplied together, not added), and we want to multiply this by a string of three a's (again, all multiplied together). How many a's would we end up with?

Let's write it out:

$$(a \times a \times a \times a \times a) \times (a \times a \times a) = a \times a \times a \times a \times a \times a \times a \times a$$

If we wrote each element of this equation exponentially, it would read:

$$a^5 \quad \times \quad a^3 \quad = \quad a^8$$ "*a* to the fifth times *a* cubed equals *a* to the eighth"

This leads us to our first rule:

1. When multiplying exponential terms that share a common base, add the exponents.

Other examples:

Exponentially	Written Out
$7^3 \times 7^2 = 7^5$	$(7 \times 7 \times 7) \times (7 \times 7) = 7 \times 7 \times 7 \times 7 \times 7$
$5 \times 5^2 \times 5^3 = 5^6$	$5 \times (5 \times 5) \times (5 \times 5 \times 5) = 5 \times 5 \times 5 \times 5 \times 5 \times 5$
$f^3 \times f^1 = f^4$	$(f \times f \times f) \times f = f \times f \times f \times f$

Now let's imagine that we are dividing a string of five a's by a string of three a's. (Again, these are strings of multiplied a's.) What would be the result?

$\dfrac{a \times a \times a \times a \times a}{a \times a \times a}$ *We can cancel out from top and bottom* $\rightarrow$ $\dfrac{a \times \cancel{a} \times \cancel{a} \times \cancel{a} \times a}{\cancel{a} \times \cancel{a} \times \cancel{a}}$ $\rightarrow$ $a \times a$

If we wrote this out exponentially, it would read

$$a^5 \quad \div \quad a^3 \quad = \quad a^2$$ "*a* to the fifth divided by *a* cubed equals *a* squared"

Which leads us to our second rule:

2. When dividing exponential terms with a common base, subtract the exponents.

Other examples:

Exponentially	Written Out
$7^5 \div 7^2 = 7^3$	$(7 \times 7 \times 7 \times 7 \times 7) / (7 \times 7) = 7 \times 7 \times 7$
$5^5 \div 5^4 = 5$	$(5 \times 5 \times 5 \times 5 \times 5) / (5 \times 5 \times 5 \times 5) = 5$
$f^4 \div f^1 = f^3$	$(f \times f \times f \times f) / (f) = f \times f \times f$

These are our first 2 exponent rules:

Rule Book: Multiplying and Dividing Like Base with Different Exponents	
When multiplying exponential terms that share a common base, add the exponents.	**When dividing exponential terms with a common base, subtract the exponents.**
$$a^3 \times a^2 = a^5$$	$$a^5 \div a^2 = a^3$$

Check Your Skills
Simplify the following expressions by combining like terms.

10. $b^5 \times b^7 =$
11. $(x^3)(x^4) =$

12. $\dfrac{y^5}{y^2} =$

13. $\dfrac{d^8}{d^7} =$

Answers can be found on page 95.

These are the most commonly used rules, but there are some other important things to know about exponents.

Additional Exponent Rules
1. When something with an exponent is raised to another power, multiply the two exponents together.

$$\left(a^2\right)^4 = a^8$$

If you have four pairs of a's, you will have a total of eight a's.

$(a \times a) \times (a \times a) \times (a \times a) \times (a \times a) = a \times a \times a \times a \times a \times a \times a \times a = a^8$

It is important to remember that the exponent rules we just discussed apply to negative exponents as well as to positive exponents. For instance, there are two ways to combine the expression $2^5 \times 2^{-3}$.

    1. The first way is to rewrite the negative exponent as a positive exponent, and then combine.

$$2^5 \times 2^{-3} = 2^5 \times \frac{1}{2^3} = \frac{2^5}{2^3} = 2^{5-3} = 2^2 = 4$$

    2. Add the exponents directly.

$$2^5 \times 2^{-3} = 2^{5+(-3)} = 2^2 = 4$$

Check Your Skills

Simplify the following expressions.

14. $(x^3)^4$

15. $(5^2)^3$

Answers can be found on page 96.

Rewriting Bases

So now you know how to combine exponential expressions when they share a common base. But what can you do when presented with an expression such as $5^3 \times 25^2$? At first, it may seem that no further simplification is possible.

The trick here is to realize that 25 is actually 5^2. Because they are equivalent values, we can replace 25 with 5^2 and see what we get.

$5^3 \times (5^2)^2$ can be rewritten as $5^3 \times 5^4$. This expression can now be combined and we end up with 5^7.

When dealing with exponential expressions, you need to be on the lookout for perfect squares and perfect cubes that can be rewritten. In our last example, 25 is a perfect square and can be rewritten as 5^2. In general, it is good to know all the perfect squares up to 15^2, the perfect cubes up to 6^3, and the powers of 2 and 3. Here's a brief list of some of the numbers likely to appear on the GRE.

    The powers of 2: 2, 4, 8, 16, 32, 64, 128
    The powers of 3: 3, 9, 27, 81

$4^2 = 16$	$10^2 = 100$	$2^3 = 8$
$5^2 = 25$	$11^2 = 121$	$3^3 = 27$
$6^2 = 36$	$12^2 = 144$	$4^3 = 64$
$7^2 = 49$	$13^2 = 169$	$5^3 = 125$
$8^2 = 64$	$14^2 = 196$	
$9^2 = 81$	$15^2 = 225$	

Let's try another example. How would you combine the expression $2^3 \times 8^4$? Try it out for yourself.

Again, the key is to recognize that 8 is 2^3. The expression can be rewritten as $2^3 \times (2^3)^4$, which becomes $2^3 \times 2^{12}$ which equals 2^{15}.

Check Your Skills
Combine the following expressions.

16. $2^4 \times 16^3$
17. $7^5 \times 49^8$
18. $9^3 \times 81^3$

Answers can be found on page 96.

Simplifying Exponential Expressions

Now that you have the basics down for working with bases and exponents, what about working with multiple exponential expressions at the same time? If two (or more) exponential terms in an expression have a base in common or an exponent in common, you can often simplify the expression. (In this section, by "simplify," we mean "reduce to one term.")

WHEN CAN YOU SIMPLIFY EXPONENTIAL EXPRESSIONS?
(1)   You can only **simplify** exponential expressions that are linked by multiplication or division. You cannot **simplify** expressions linked by addition or subtraction (although in some cases, you can **factor** them and otherwise manipulate them).
(2)   You can simplify exponential expressions linked by multiplication or division if they have either a base or an exponent in common.

HOW CAN YOU SIMPLIFY THEM?
Use the exponent rules described earlier. If you forget these rules, you can derive them on the test by writing out the example exponential expressions.

These expressions CANNOT be simplified:	**These expressions CAN be simplified:**
$7^4 + 7^6$	$(7^4)(7^6)$
$3^4 + 12^4$	$(3^4)(12^4)$
$6^5 - 6^3$	$\dfrac{6^5}{6^3}$
$12^7 - 3^7$	$\dfrac{12^7}{3^7}$

Use the rules outlined above to simplify the expressions in the right column:

$$(7^4)(7^6) = 7^{4+6} = 7^{10} \qquad\qquad \frac{6^5}{6^3} = 6^{5-3} = 6^2$$

$$(3^4)(12^4) = (3 \times 12)^4 = 36^4 \qquad\qquad \frac{12^7}{3^7} = \left(\frac{12}{3}\right)^7 = 4^7$$

We can simplify all the expressions in the right-hand column to a single term, because the terms are multiplied or divided. The expressions in the left-hand column **cannot be simplified**, because the terms are added or subtracted. However, they **can be factored** whenever the base is the same. For example, $7^4 + 7^6$ can be factored because the two terms in the expression have a factor in common. What factor exactly do they have in common? Both terms contain 7^4. If we factor 7^4 out of each term, we are left with $7^4(7^2 + 1) = 7^4(50)$.

The terms can ALSO be factored whenever the exponent is the same and the terms contain something in common in the base. For example, $3^4 + 12^4$ can be factored because $12^4 = (2 \times 2 \times 3)^4$. Thus both bases contain 3^4, and the factored expression is $3^4(1 + 4^4)$.

Likewise, $6^5 - 6^3$ can be factored as $6^3(6^2 - 1)$ and $12^7 - 3^7$ can be factored as $3^7(4^7 - 1)$.

On the GRE, it generally pays to factor exponential terms that have something in common in the bases.

> If $x = 4^{20} + 4^{21} + 4^{22}$, what is the largest prime factor of x?

All three terms contain 4^{20}, so we can factor the expression: $x = 4^{20}(4^0 + 4^1 + 4^2)$. Therefore, $x = 4^{20}(1 + 4 + 16) = 4^{20}(21) = 4^{20}(3 \times 7)$. The largest prime factor of x is 7.

Rules of Exponents

Exponent Rule	Examples
$x^a \cdot x^b = x^{a+b}$	$c^3 \cdot c^5 = c^8 \qquad 3^5 \cdot 3^8 = 3^{13}$ $5(5^n) = 5^1(5^n) = 5^{n+1}$
$a^x \cdot b^x = (ab)^x$	$2^4 \cdot 3^4 = 6^4 \qquad 12^5 = 2^{10} \cdot 3^5$
$\dfrac{x^a}{x^b} = x^{(a-b)}$	$\dfrac{2^5}{2^{11}} = \dfrac{1}{2^6} = 2^{-6} \qquad \dfrac{x^{10}}{x^3} = x^7$
$\left(\dfrac{a}{b}\right)^x = \dfrac{a^x}{b^x}$	$\left(\dfrac{10}{2}\right)^6 = \dfrac{10^6}{2^6} = 5^6 \qquad \dfrac{3^5}{9^5} = \left(\dfrac{3}{9}\right)^5 = \left(\dfrac{1}{3}\right)^5$
$(a^x)^y = a^{xy} = (a^y)^x$	$(3^2)^4 = 3^{2 \cdot 4} = 3^8 = 3^{4 \cdot 2} = (3^4)^2$
$x^{-a} = \dfrac{1}{x^a}$	$\left(\dfrac{3}{2}\right)^{-2} = \left(\dfrac{2}{3}\right)^2 = \dfrac{4}{9} \qquad 2x^{-4} = \dfrac{2}{x^4}$
$a^x + a^x + a^x = 3a^x$	$3^4 + 3^4 + 3^4 = 3 \cdot 3^4 = 3^5$ $3^x + 3^x + 3^x = 3 \cdot 3^x = 3^{x+1}$

Check Your Skills

19. Which of these expressions can be simplified?
    a. $x^2 + x^2$
    b. $x^2 \cdot y^2$
    c. $2(2^n + 3^n)$

The answer can be found on page 96.

Common Exponent Errors

Study this list of common errors carefully and identify any mistakes that you occasionally make. Note the numerical examples given!

INCORRECT	**CORRECT**
$(x + y)^2 = x^2 + y^2$? $(3 + 2)^2 = 3^2 + 2^2 = 13$?	$(x + y)^2 = x^2 + 2xy + y^2$ $(3 + 2)^2 = 5^2 = 25$
$a^x \cdot b^y = (ab)^{x+y}$? $2^4 \cdot 3^5 = (2 \cdot 3)^{4+5}$?	Cannot be simplified further (different bases **and** different exponents)
$a^x \cdot a^y = a^{xy}$? $5^4 \cdot 5^3 = 5^{12}$?	$a^x \cdot a^y = a^{x+y}$ $5^4 \cdot 5^3 = 5^7$
$(a^x)^y = a^{(x+y)}$? $(7^4)^3 = 7^7$?	$(a^x)^y = a^{xy}$ $(7^4)^3 = 7^{12}$
$a^x + a^y = a^{x+y}$? $x^3 + x^2 = x^5$?	Cannot be simplified further (addition **and** different exponents)
$a^x + a^x = a^{2x}$? $2^x + 2^x = 2^{2x}$?	$a^x + a^x = 2a^x$ $2^x + 2^x = 2(2^x) = 2^{x+1}$
$a \cdot a^x = a^{2x}$? $5 \cdot 5^z = 25^z$?	$a \cdot a^x = a^{x+1}$ $5 \cdot 5^z = 5^{z+1}$
$-x^2 = x^2$? $-4^2 = 16$?	$-x^2$ cannot be simplified further $-4^2 = -16$ **Compare:** $(-x)^2 = x^2$ **and** $(-4)^2 = 16$
$a \cdot b^x = (a \cdot b)^x$? $2 \cdot 3^4 = (2 \cdot 3)^4$?	Cannot be simplified further

Check Your Skills Answer Key:

1. **−3:** If a number is raised to an odd power ($x \cdot x \cdot x = x^3$), the result will have the same sign as the original base. This means that x must be −3.

2. **2 or −2:** We have an even power here ($x^2 \cdot x^3 \cdot x = x^6$), so the base could be positive or negative. This means x could be either 2 or −2.

3. **1:** Whenever you multiply two terms with the same base, add the exponents. $4 + (−4) = 0$, and $x^0 = 1$. This means $y = 1$.

4. **1, −1:** Remember that you can't simply subtract the exponents here and get $x^2 = 0$ (this would lead us to believe that $x = 0$, which we'll soon see it couldn't be, because the second equation wouldn't work). Instead, our rules tell us that if $x^3 = x$ (which we get if we add x to both sides of the first equation), x can be 0 *or* 1. If $x = 1$, our second equation works as well, so $x = 1$.

5. **(0.8)²:** Every fraction gets smaller the higher you raise its power, so both of these will get smaller. They will also get smaller at a faster rate depending on how small they already are. $\dfrac{3}{4} = 0.75$, which is smaller than 0.8. This means that $(0.75)^2 < (0.8)^2$. You can also think of it this way: 75% of 75 will be smaller than 80% of 80.

6. $\left(\dfrac{\mathbf{10}}{\mathbf{7}}\right)^{\mathbf{2}}$ **:** Even though $\dfrac{10}{7}$ is being presented to you in fractional form, it is an improper fraction, meaning its value

is greater than 1. When something greater than 1 is raised to a power, it gets bigger. This means that $\left(\dfrac{10}{7}\right)^2 > \dfrac{10}{7}$.

7. **3:** Quick thinking about powers of 2 should lead us to $2^4 = 16$. The equation can be rewritten as $2^1 \cdot 2^x = 2^4$. Now we can ignore the bases, because the powers should add up: $x + 1 = 4$, so $x = 3$.

8. **1:** Anything raised to the 0 power equals 1, so the expression on the left side of this equation must be equivalent to 5^0. When dividing terms with the same base, subtract exponents.

$$5^{y+2-3} = 5^0.$$

Now ignore the bases: $y + 2 − 3 = 0$, so $y = 1$.

9. **1:** $\dfrac{1}{2}$ can be rewritten as 2^{-1}, and $\dfrac{1}{4}$ can be rewritten as 2^{-2}, so our equation becomes $2^{-y} = 2^{(y-2)}$. Now we can ignore the powers, so $−y = y − 2$.

$$2y = 2, \text{ and } y = 1.$$

10. $b^5 \times b^7 = b^{(5+7)} = b^{12}$
11. $(x^3)(x^4) = x^{(3+4)} = x^7$
12. $\dfrac{y^5}{y^2} = y^{(5-2)} = y^3$

13. $\dfrac{d^8}{d^7} = d^{(8-7)} = d$

14. $(x^3)^4 = x^{3 \times 4} = x^{12}$

15. $(5^2)^3 = 5^{2 \times 3} = 5^6$

16. $2^4 \times 16^3 = 2^4 \times (2^4)^3 = 2^4 \times 2^{4 \times 3} = 2^4 \times 2^{12} = 2^{4+12} = 2^{16}$

17. $7^5 \times 49^8 = 7^5 \times (7^2)^8 = 7^5 \times 7^{2 \times 8} = 7^5 \times 7^{16} = 7^{5+16} = 7^{21}$

18. $9^3 \times 81^3 = (3^2)^3 \times (3^4)^3 = 3^{2 \times 3} \times 3^{4 \times 3} = 3^6 \times 3^{12} = 3^{6+12} = 3^{18}$

19.

    a.   This cannot be simplified, except to say $2x^2$. We can't combine the bases or powers in any more interesting way.

    b.   Even though we have two different variables here, our rules hold, and we can multiply the bases and maintain the power: $(xy)^2$.

    c.   Half of this expression can be simplified, namely the part that involves the common base, 2: $2^{n+1} + 2 \times 3^n$. It may not be much prettier, but at least we've joined up the common terms.

Problem Set

Simplify or otherwise reduce the following expressions using the rules of exponents.

1. 2^{-5}

2. $\dfrac{7^6}{7^4}$

3. $8^4(5^4)$

4. $2^4 \times 2^5 \div 2^7 - 2^4$

5. $\dfrac{9^4}{3^4} + \left(4^2\right)^3$

Solve the following problems.

6. Does $a^2 + a^4 = a^6$ for all values of a?

7. $x^3 < x^2$. Describe the possible values of x.

8. If $x^4 = 16$, what is $|x|$?

9. If $y^5 > 0$, is $y < 0$?

10. If $b > a > 0$, and $c \neq 0$, is $a^2 b^3 c^4$ positive?

11. Simplify: $\dfrac{y^2 \times y^5}{(y^2)^4}$

12. If $r^3 + |r| = 0$, what are the possible values of r?

13.

Quantity A	Quantity B
2^y	$\left(\dfrac{1}{2}\right)^{-y}$

14.

Quantity A	Quantity B
$3^3 \cdot 9^6 \cdot 2^4 \cdot 4^2$	$9^3 \cdot 3^6 \cdot 2^2 \cdot 4^4$

15.

$$y > 1$$

Quantity A	Quantity B
$(0.99)^y$	$0.99 \cdot y$

1. $\dfrac{1}{32}$: Remember that a negative exponent yields the reciprocal of the same expression with a positive exponent. $2^{-5} = \dfrac{1}{2^5} = \dfrac{1}{32}$

2. **49:** $\dfrac{7^6}{7^4} = 7^{6-4} = 7^2 = 49$

3. **40^4:** $8^4(5^4) = 40^4$

4. **−12:** $\dfrac{2^4 \times 2^5}{2^7} - 2^4 = 2^{(4+5-7)} - 2^4 = 2^2 - 2^4 = 2^2(1 - 2^2) = 4(1 - 4) = -12.$

5. **4,177:** $\dfrac{9^4}{3^4} + \left(4^2\right)^3 = 3^4 + 4^6 = 81 + 4{,}096 = 4{,}177$

6. **NO:** Remember, you cannot combine exponential expressions linked by addition.

7. **Any non-zero number less than 1:** As positive proper fractions are multiplied, their value decreases. For example, $\left(\dfrac{1}{2}\right)^3 < \left(\dfrac{1}{2}\right)^2$. Also, any negative number will make this inequality true. A negative number cubed is negative. Any negative number squared is positive. For example, $(-3)^3 < (-3)^2$. The number zero itself, however, does not work, since $0^3 = 0^2$.

8. **2:** The possible values for x are 2 and −2. The absolute value of both 2 and −2 is 2.

9. **NO:** An integer raised to an odd exponent retains the original sign of the base. Therefore, if y^5 is positive, y is positive.

10. **YES:** b and a are both positive numbers. Whether c is positive or negative, c^4 is positive. (Recall that any number raised to an even power is positive.) Therefore, the product $a^2b^3c^4$ is the product of 3 positive numbers, which will be positive.

11. $\dfrac{1}{y}$: $\dfrac{y^2 \times y^5}{(y^2)^4} = \dfrac{y^7}{y^8} = y^{7-8} = y^{-1} = \dfrac{1}{y}$

12. **0,−1:** If $r^3 + |r| = 0$, then r^3 must be the opposite of $|r|$. The only values for which this would be true are 0, which is the opposite of itself, and −1, whose opposite is 1.

13. **C:** When you raise a number to a negative power, that's the same as raising its reciprocal to the positive version of that power. For instance, $3^{-2} = \left(\dfrac{1}{3}\right)^2$, because $\dfrac{1}{3}$ is the reciprocal of 3. The reciprocal of $\dfrac{1}{2}$ is 2, so Quantity B can be rewritten.

Quantity A	**Quantity B**
2^y	$\left(\dfrac{1}{2}\right)^{-y} = (2)^y$

Therefore **the two quantities are equal.**

14. **A:** The goal with exponent questions is always to get the same bases, the simplest versions of which will always be prime. Each Quantity has the same four bases: 2, 3, 4 and 9. 2 and 3 are already prime, so we need to manipulate 4 and 9. $4 = 2^2$ and $9 = 3^2$. Rewrite the quantities.

Quantity A	**Quantity B**
$3^3 \cdot 9^6 \cdot 2^4 \cdot 4^2 =$	$9^3 \cdot 3^6 \cdot 2^2 \cdot 4^4 =$
$3^3 \cdot (3^2)^6 \cdot 2^4 \cdot (2^2)^2$	$(3^2)^3 \cdot 3^6 \cdot 2^2 \cdot (2^2)^4$

Now terms can be combined using the exponent rules.

Quantity A	**Quantity B**
$3^3 \cdot (3^2)^6 \cdot 2^4 \cdot (2^2)^2 =$	$(3^2)^3 \cdot 3^6 \cdot 2^2 \cdot (2^2)^4 =$
$3^3 \cdot 3^{12} \cdot 2^4 \cdot 2^4 =$	$3^6 \cdot 3^6 \cdot 2^2 \cdot 2^8 =$
$3^{15} \cdot 2^8$	$3^{12} \cdot 2^{10}$

Now divide away common terms. Both quantities contain the product $3^{12} \cdot 2^8$.

Quantity A	**Quantity B**
$\dfrac{3^{15} \cdot 2^8}{3^{12} \cdot 2^8} = 3^3 = 27$	$\dfrac{3^{12} \cdot 2^{10}}{3^{12} \cdot 2^8} = 2^2 = 4$

Therefore **Quantity A is larger.**

15. **B:** Any number less than one raised to a power greater than 1 will get smaller, so even though we don't know the value of y, we do know that the value in Quantity A will be less than 0.99.

$$y > 1$$

Quantity A	**Quantity B**
$(0.99)^y \rightarrow$ less than 0.99	$0.99 \cdot y$

Conversely, any positive number multiplied by a number greater than 1 will get bigger. We don't know the value in Quantity B, but we know that it will be larger than 0.99

$$y > 1$$

Quantity A	**Quantity B**
$(0.99)^y \rightarrow$ less than 0.99	$0.99 \cdot y \rightarrow$ greater than 0.99

Therefore **Quantity B is larger.**

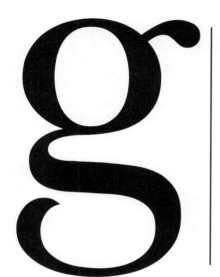

Chapter 6
of
NUMBER PROPERTIES

ROOTS

In This Chapter . . .

Basic Properties of Roots

Now we're going to discuss some of the ways roots are incorporated into expressions and equations and the ways we are allowed to manipulate them. You may be tempted to use the on-screen calculator when you see a root expression, but it's often much easier to go without. You just need to know your roots rules!

Before getting into some of the more complicated rules, it is important to remember that any square root times itself will equal whatever is inside the square root. For instance, $\sqrt{2} \times \sqrt{2} = 2$. $\sqrt{18} \times \sqrt{18} = 18$. We can even apply this rule to variables: $\sqrt{y} \times \sqrt{y} = y$. So our first rule for roots is:

$$\sqrt{x} \times \sqrt{x} = x$$

Multiplication and Division of Roots

Suppose you were to see the equation $3 + \sqrt{4} = x$, and you were asked to solve for x. What would you do? Well, $\sqrt{4} = 2$, so you could rewrite the equation as $3 + 2 = x$, so you would know that $x = 5$. 4 is a perfect square, so we were able to simply evaluate the root, and continue to solve the problem. But what if the equation were $\sqrt{8} \times \sqrt{2} = x$, and you were asked to find x. What would you do then? Neither 8 nor 2 is a perfect square, so we can't easily find a value for either root.

It is important to realize that, on the GRE, sometimes you will be able to evaluate roots, (when asked to take the square root of a perfect square or the cube root of a perfect cube) but other times it will be necessary to manipulate the roots. We'll discuss the different ways that we are allowed to manipulate roots, and then see some examples of how these manipulations may help us arrive at a correct answer on GRE questions involving roots.

Let's go back to the previous question. If $\sqrt{8} \times \sqrt{2} = x$, what is x?

When two roots are multiplied by each other, we can do the multiplication within a single root. What that means is that we can rewrite $\sqrt{8} \times \sqrt{2}$ as $\sqrt{8 \times 2}$, which equals $\sqrt{16}$. And $\sqrt{16}$ equals 4, which means that $x = 4$.

This property also works for division.

If $x = \dfrac{\sqrt{27}}{\sqrt{3}}$, what is x?

We can divide the numbers inside the square roots and put them inside one square root. So $\dfrac{\sqrt{27}}{\sqrt{3}}$ becomes $\sqrt{\dfrac{27}{3}}$ which becomes $\sqrt{9}$. And $\sqrt{9}$ equals 3, so $x = 3$.

Note that these rules apply if there are any number of roots being multiplied or divided. These rules can also be combined with each other. For instance, $\dfrac{\sqrt{15} \times \sqrt{12}}{\sqrt{5}}$ becomes $\sqrt{\dfrac{15 \times 12}{5}}$. The numbers inside can be combined, and ultimately you end up with $\sqrt{36}$, which equals 6.

Check Your Skills

Solve for x.

1. $x = \sqrt{20} \times \sqrt{5}$

2. $x = \sqrt{20} \div \sqrt{5}$

3. $x = \sqrt{2} \times \sqrt{6} \times \sqrt{12}$

4. $x = \dfrac{\sqrt{384}}{\sqrt{2} \times \sqrt{3}}$

Answers can be found on page 107.

Simplifying Roots

Just as multiple roots can be combined to create one root, we can also take one root and break it apart into multiple roots. You may be asking, why would we ever want to do that? Well, suppose a question said, if $x = \sqrt{2} \times \sqrt{6}$, what is x? You would combine them, and say that x equals $\sqrt{12}$. Unfortunately, $\sqrt{12}$ will never be a correct answer on the GRE. The reason is that $\sqrt{12}$ can be simplified, and correct answers on the GRE are presented in their simplest forms. So now the question becomes, how can we simplify $\sqrt{12}$?

What if we were to rewrite $\sqrt{12}$ as $\sqrt{4 \times 3}$? As mentioned, we could also break this apart into two separate roots that are multiplied together, namely $\sqrt{4} \times \sqrt{3}$. And we already know that $\sqrt{4}$ equals 2, so we could simplify to $2\sqrt{3}$. And in fact, that is the simplified form of $\sqrt{12}$, and could potentially appear as the correct answer to a question on the GRE. Just to recap, the progression of simplifying $\sqrt{12}$, was as follows:

$$\sqrt{12} \rightarrow \sqrt{4 \times 3} \rightarrow \sqrt{4} \times \sqrt{3} \rightarrow 2\sqrt{3}$$

Now the question becomes, how can we simplify *any* square root? What if we don't notice that 12 equals 4 times 3, and 4 is a perfect square? Amazingly enough, the method for simplifying square roots will involve something you're probably quite comfortable with at this point—prime factorizations.

Take a look at the prime factorization of 12. The prime factorization of 12 is $2 \times 2 \times 3$. So $\sqrt{12}$ can be rewritten as $\sqrt{2 \times 2 \times 3}$. Recall our first roots rule—any root times itself will equal the number inside. If $\sqrt{12}$ can be rewritten as $\sqrt{2 \times 2 \times 3}$, we can take that one step further and say it is $\sqrt{2} \times \sqrt{2} \times \sqrt{3}$. And we know that $\sqrt{2} \times \sqrt{2} = 2$.

We can generalize from this example and say that when we take the prime factorization of a number inside a square root, any prime factor that we can pair off can effectively be brought out of the square root. Let's try another example to practice applying this concept. What is the simplified form of $\sqrt{360}$? Let's start by taking the prime factorization of 360.

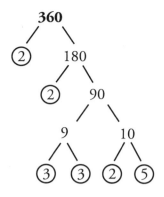

$$360 = 2 \times 2 \times 2 \times 3 \times 3 \times 5$$

Again, we are looking for primes that we can pair off and ultimately remove from the square root. In this case, we have a pair of 2's and a pair of 3's, so let's separate them.

$$\sqrt{360} \rightarrow \sqrt{2 \times 2 \times 2 \times 3 \times 3 \times 5} \rightarrow \sqrt{2 \times 2} \times \sqrt{3 \times 3} \rightarrow \sqrt{2 \times 5}$$

Notice that the prime factorization of 360 included three 2's. Two 2's could be paired off, but that still left one 2 without a partner. $\sqrt{2 \times 5}$ represents the prime factors that cannot be paired off. This expression can now be simplified to $2 \times 3 \times \sqrt{2 \times 5}$ which is $6\sqrt{10}$.

You might have seen right away that $360 = 36 \times 10$, so $\sqrt{360} = \sqrt{36 \times 10} = \sqrt{36} \times \sqrt{10} = 6\sqrt{10}$. The advantage of the prime factor method is that it will always work, even when you don't spot a shortcut.

Check Your Skills
Simplify the following roots.

5. $\sqrt{75}$

6. $\sqrt{96}$

7. $\sqrt{441}$

Answers can be found on page 107.

Solving Algebraic Equations Involving Exponential Terms

GRE exponent problems sometimes give you an equation, and ask you to solve for either an unknown base, or an unknown exponent.

Unknown Base

The key to solving algebraic expressions with an unknown base is to make use of the fact that exponents and roots can effectively cancel each other out. In the equation $x^3 = 8$, x is raised to the third power, so to eliminate the exponent we can take the cube root of both sides of the equation.

$$\sqrt[3]{x^3} = x \quad \text{SO} \quad \sqrt[3]{8} = 2 = x$$

This process also works in reverse. If we are presented with the equation $\sqrt{x} = 6$, we can eliminate the square root by squaring both sides. Square root and squaring cancel each other out in the same way that cube root and raising something to the third power cancel each other out. So to solve this equation, we can square both sides and get $(\sqrt{x})^2 = 6^2$, which can be simplified to $x = 36$.

There is one additional danger. Remember that when solving an equation where a variable has been squared, you should be on the lookout for two solutions. To solve for y in the equation $y^2 = 100$, we need to remember that y can equal either 10 OR -10.

Unknown Base	Unknown Exponent
$x^3 = 8$	$2^x = 8$

Check Your Skills
Solve the following equations.

8. $x^3 = 64$

9. $\sqrt[3]{x} = 6$

10. $x^2 = 121$

Answers can be found on page 107.

Unknown Exponent

Unlike examples in the previous section, we can't make use of the relationship between exponents and roots to help us solve for a variable in the equation $2^x = 8$. Instead, the key is to once again recognize that 8 is equivalent to 2^3, and rewrite the equation so that we have the same base on both sides of the equal sign. If we replace 8 with its equivalent value, the equation becomes $2^x = 2^3$.

Now that we have the same base on both sides of the equation, there is only one way for the value of the expression on the left side of the equation to equal the value of the expression on the right side of the equation—the exponents must be equal. We can effectively ignore the bases and set the exponents equal to each other. We now know that $x = 3$.

By the way, when you see the expression 2^x, always call it "two TO THE xth power" or "two TO THE x." Never call it "two x." "Two x" is $2x$, or 2 times x, which is simply a different expression. Don't get lazy with names; that's how you can confuse one expression for another.

The process of finding the same base on each side of the equation can be applied to more complicated exponents as well. Take a look at the equation $3^{x+2} = 27$. Once again, we must first rewrite one of the bases so that the bases are the same on both sides of the equation. 27 is equivalent to 3^3, so the equation can be rewritten as $3^{x+2} = 3^3$. We can now ignore the bases (because they are the same) and set the exponents equal to each other.

$x + 2 = 3$, which means that $x = 1$.

Check Your Skills
Solve for x in the following equations.

11. $2^x = 64$

12. $7^{x-2} = 49$

13. $5^{3x} = 125$

Answers can be found on page 107.

Check Your Skills Answer Key:

1. $x = \sqrt{20} \times \sqrt{5} = \sqrt{20 \times 5} = \sqrt{100} = 10$

2. $x = \dfrac{\sqrt{20}}{\sqrt{5}} = \sqrt{\dfrac{20}{5}} = \sqrt{4} = 2$

3. $x = \sqrt{2} \times \sqrt{6} \times \sqrt{12} = \sqrt{2 \times 6 \times 12} = \sqrt{144} = 12$

4. $x = \dfrac{\sqrt{384}}{\sqrt{2} \times \sqrt{3}} = \sqrt{\dfrac{384}{2 \times 3}} = \sqrt{\dfrac{384}{6}} = \sqrt{64} = 8$

5. $\sqrt{75} \rightarrow \sqrt{3 \times 5 \times 5} \rightarrow \sqrt{5 \times 5} \times \sqrt{3} = 5\sqrt{3}$

6. $\sqrt{96} = \sqrt{2 \times 2 \times 2 \times 2 \times 2 \times 3} = \sqrt{2 \times 2} \times \sqrt{2 \times 2} \times \sqrt{2 \times 3} = 2 \times 2 \times \sqrt{6} = 4\sqrt{6}$

7. $\sqrt{441} \rightarrow \sqrt{3 \times 3 \times 7 \times 7} \rightarrow \sqrt{3 \times 3} \times \sqrt{7 \times 7} = 3 \times 7 = 21$

8. $x^3 = 64$

   $\sqrt[3]{x^3} = \sqrt[3]{64}$

   $x = 4$

9. $\sqrt[3]{x} = 6$

   $(\sqrt[3]{x})^3 = (6)^3$

   $x = 216$

10. $x^2 = 121$

   $\sqrt{x^2} = \sqrt{121}$

   $x = 11 \quad \text{OR} \quad -11$

11. $2^x = 64$

   $2^x = 2^6$

   $x = 6$

12. $7^{x-2} = 49$

   $7^{x-2} = 7^2$

   $x - 2 = 2$

   $x = 4$

13. $5^{3x} = 125$

   $5^{3x} = 5^3$

   $3x = 3$

   $x = 1$

Problem Set

1.

Quantity A	**Quantity B**

$$\sqrt{30} \times \sqrt{5}$$ 12

2.

$$36 < x < 49$$

Quantity A	**Quantity B**

$$2^{\sqrt{x}}$$ $$4^3$$

3.

Quantity A	**Quantity B**

$$\frac{\sqrt{6} \times \sqrt{18}}{\sqrt{9}}$$ $$\frac{\sqrt{8} \times \sqrt{12}}{\sqrt{6}}$$

1. **A:** One of our root rules is that when two individual roots are multiplied together, we can carry out that multiplication under a single root sign.

$$\sqrt{30} \times \sqrt{5} = \sqrt{30 \times 5} = \sqrt{150}$$

While this can be simplified $(\sqrt{150} = \sqrt{25 \times 6} = 5\sqrt{6},)$ we're actually better off leaving it as is.

Quantity A	**Quantity B**
$\sqrt{30} \times \sqrt{5} = \sqrt{150}$	12

Now square both quantities.

Quantity A	**Quantity B**
$(\sqrt{150})^2 = 150$	$(12)^2 = 144$

Quantity A is larger.

2. **A:** The common information tells you that x is between 36 and 49, which means the square root of x must be between 6 and 7. Rewrite Quantity A.

$$36 < x < 49$$

Quantity A	**Quantity B**
$2^6 < 2^{\sqrt{x}} < 2^7$	4^3

Now rewrite Quantity B so that it has a base of 2 instead of a base of 4.

$$36 < x < 49$$

Quantity A	**Quantity B**
$2^6 < 2^{\sqrt{x}} < 2^7$	$4^3 = (2^2)^3 = 2^6$

The value in **Quantity A must be greater** than 2^6, and so must be greater than the value in Quantity B.

3. **B:** Simplify both quantities by combining the roots into one root.

Quantity A	**Quantity B**
$$\sqrt{\dfrac{6 \times 18}{9}} =$$	$$\sqrt{\dfrac{8 \times 12}{6}} =$$
$$\sqrt{\dfrac{6 \times \cancel{18}^{\,2}}{\cancel{9}_{\,1}}} = \sqrt{12}$$	$$\sqrt{\dfrac{8 \times \cancel{12}^{\,2}}{\cancel{6}_{\,1}}} = \sqrt{16}$$

Now simplify the fractions underneath each root.

$\sqrt{16}$ is larger than $\sqrt{12}$.

Quantity B is greater.

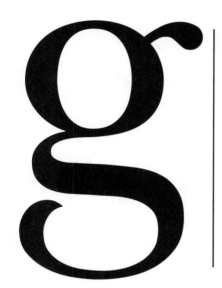

Chapter 7
of
NUMBER PROPERTIES

CONSECUTIVE
INTEGERS

In This Chapter . . .

CONSECUTIVE INTEGERS

Consecutive integers are integers that follow one after another from a given starting point, without skipping any integers. For example, 4, 5, 6, and 7 are consecutive integers, but 4, 6, 7, and 9 are not. There are many other types of related consecutive patterns. For example:

Consecutive Even Integers: 8, 10, 12, 14
(8, 10, 14, and 16 is incorrect, as it skips 12)

Consecutive Primes: 11, 13, 17, 19
(11, 13, 15, and 17 is wrong, as 15 is not prime)

Evenly Spaced Sets

To understand consecutive integers, we should first consider sets of **evenly spaced sets**. These are sequences of numbers whose values go up or down by the same amount (the **increment**) from one item in the sequence to the next. For instance, the set {4, 7, 10, 13, 16} is evenly spaced because each value increases by 3 over the previous value.

Sets of **consecutive multiples** are special cases of evenly spaced sets: all of the values in the set are multiples of the increment. For example, {12, 16, 20, 24} is a set of consecutive multiples because the values increase from one to the next by 4, and each element is a multiple of 4. Note that sets of consecutive multiples *must* be composed of integers.

Sets of **consecutive integers** are special cases of consecutive multiples: all of the values in the set increase by 1, and all integers are multiples of 1. For example, {12, 13, 14, 15, 16} is a set of consecutive integers because the values increase from one to the next by 1, and each element is an integer.

The relations among evenly spaced sets, consecutive multiples, and consecutive integers are displayed in the diagram to the right:

- All sets of consecutive integers are sets of consecutive multiples.
- All sets of consecutive multiples are evenly spaced sets.
- All evenly spaced sets are fully defined if the following 3 parameters are known:

  (1) The smallest (**first**) or largest (**last**) number in the set

  (2) The **increment** (always 1 for consecutive integers)

  (3) The **number of items** in the set.

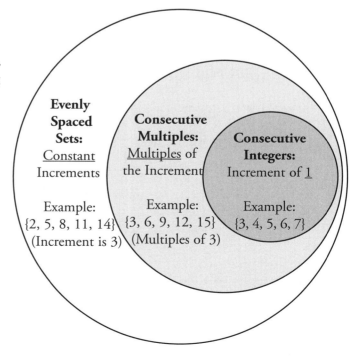

Evenly Spaced Sets:
Constant Increments

Example:
{2, 5, 8, 11, 14}
(Increment is 3)

Consecutive Multiples:
Multiples of the Increment

Example:
{3, 6, 9, 12, 15}
(Multiples of 3)

Consecutive Integers:
Increment of 1

Example:
{3, 4, 5, 6, 7}

Check Your Skills

1. Which of the following are evenly spaced sets?
   a. $\sqrt{1}, \sqrt{2}, \sqrt{3}, \sqrt{4}, \sqrt{5}$
   b. $x, x - 4, x - 8, x - 12, x - 16$
   c. $\sqrt{4}, \sqrt{9}, \sqrt{16}, \sqrt{25}, \sqrt{36}$
   d. $5^1, 5^2, 5^3, 5^4, 5^5$
   e. $y, 2y, 3y, 4y, 5y$

Answers can be found on page 119.

Properties of Evenly Spaced Sets

The following properties apply to **all** evenly spaced sets. However, just because a set has these properties does not necessarily mean that the set is evenly spaced.

(1)   The **arithmetic mean** (average) and **median** are equal to each other. In other words, the average of the elements in the set can be found by figuring out the median, or "middle number."

   What is the arithmetic mean of 4, 8, 12, 16, and 20?

In this example we have 5 consecutive multiples of four. The median is the 3rd largest, or 12. Since this is an evenly spaced set, the arithmetic mean (average) is also 12.

   What is the arithmetic mean of 4, 8, 12, 16, 20, and 24?

In this example we have 6 consecutive multiples of four. The median is the arithmetic mean (average) of the 3rd largest and 4th largest, or the average of 12 and 16. Thus the median is 14. Since this is an evenly spaced set, the average is also 14.

(2)   The **mean** and **median** of the set are equal to the **average** of the FIRST and LAST terms.

   What is the arithmetic mean of 4, 8, 12, 16, and 20?

In this example, 20 is the largest (last) number and 4 is the smallest (first). The arithmetic mean and median are therefore equal to (20 + 4) ÷ 2 = 12.

   What is the arithmetic mean of 4, 8, 12, 16, 20, and 24?

In this example, 24 is the largest (last) number and 4 is the smallest (first). The arithmetic mean and median are therefore equal to (24 + 4) ÷ 2 = 14.

Thus for all evenly spaced sets, just remember: the average equals (**First** + **Last**) ÷ **2**.

(3)   The **sum** of the elements in the set equals the **arithmetic mean** (average) times the **number of items** in the set.

This property applies to all sets, but it takes on special significance in the case of evenly spaced sets because the "average" is not only the arithmetic mean, but also the median.

What is the sum of 4, 8, 12, 16, and 20?

We have already calculated the average above; it is equal to 12. There are 5 terms, so the sum equals $12 \times 5 = 60$.

What is the sum of 4, 8, 12, 16, 20, and 24?

We have already calculated the average above; it is equal to 14. There are 6 terms, so the sum equals $14 \times 6 = 84$.

Check Your Skills

2. What is the sum of the numbers 13, 14, 15, and 16?
3. If $x = 3$, what is the sum of $2x$, $(2x + 1)$, $(2x + 2)$, $(2x + 3)$, and $(2x + 4)$?

Answers can be found on page 119.

Counting Integers: Add One Before You Are Done

How many integers are there from 6 to 10? Four, right? Wrong! There are actually five integers from 6 to 10. Count them and you will see: 6, 7, 8, 9, 10. It is easy to forget that you have to include extremes. In this case, both extremes (the numbers 6 and 10) must be counted.

Do you have to methodically count each term in a long consecutive pattern? No. Just remember that if both extremes should be counted, you need to take the difference of the last and first numbers and **add one before you are done**.

How many integers are there from 14 to 765, inclusive?

$765 - 14$, plus 1, yields 752.

Just remember: for consecutive integers, the formula is (**Last − First + 1**).

This works easily enough if you are dealing with consecutive integers. Sometimes, however, the question will ask about consecutive multiples. For example, "How many multiples of 4..." or "How many even numbers..." are examples of sets of consecutive multiples.

In this case, if we just subtract the largest number from the smallest and add one, we will be overcounting. For example, "All of the even integers between 12 and 24" yields 12, 14, 16, 18, 20, 22, and 24. That is 7 even integers. However, (Last − First + 1) would yield $(24 − 12 + 1) = 13$, which is too large. How do we amend this? Since the items in the list are going up by increments of 2 (we are counting only the even numbers), we need to divide (Last − First) by 2. Then, add the one before you are done:

(Last − First) ÷ Increment + 1 = $(24 − 12) ÷ 2 + 1 = 6 + 1 = 7$.

Just remember: for consecutive multiples, the formula is (**Last − First**) ÷ **Increment + 1**. The bigger the increment, the smaller the result, because there is a larger gap between the numbers you are counting.

Sometimes, however, it is easier to list the terms of a consecutive pattern and count them, especially if the list is short or if one or both of the extremes are omitted.

How many multiples of 7 are there between 100 and 150?

Note that the first and last items in the set are omitted—they must be determined by you. Here it may be easiest to list the multiples: 105, 112, 119, 126, 133, 140, 147. Count the number of terms to get the answer: 7. Alternatively, we could note that 105 is the first number, 147 is the last number, and 7 is the increment:

Number of terms = (Last − First) ÷ Increment + 1 = (147 − 105) ÷ 7 + 1 = 6 + 1 = 7.

Check Your Skills

4. How many integers are there from 1,002 to 10,001?
5. How many multiples of 11 are there between 55 and 144, exclusive?

Answers can be found on page 119.

Check Your Skills Answer Key

1.
   a. **Not evenly spaced:** Even though the number inside the square root is going up by the same interval every time, the actual value is not. For example, $\sqrt{1}=1$ and $\sqrt{2}=$ approximately 1.4. That's a difference of 0.4. But $\sqrt{3}=$ approximately 1.7. and $\sqrt{4}=2$. That's a difference of 0.3. Because the interval is changing, this is not an evenly spaced set.
   b. **Evenly spaced:** No matter what x is, this set will end up being evenly spaced. For example, if x were 3, $x-4$ would equal -1, which is a difference of 4. Then $x-8$ would equal -5 and $x-12$ would equal -9, which is also a difference of 4. The interval is unchanged, so this is an evenly spaced set.
   c. **Evenly spaced:** This is the opposite of example a. In this case, the terms inside the square root signs are not creating an evenly spaced set, but the actual values are. $\sqrt{4}=2$, and $\sqrt{9}=3$. That's a difference of one. $\sqrt{16}=4$, and $\sqrt{25}=5$. That's a difference of one. The interval is unchanged, so this is an evenly spaced set (and a set of consecutive integers at that).
   d. **Not evenly spaced:** $5^1=5$ and $5^2=25$. That's a difference of 20. But $5^3=125$, which is 100 larger than the previous term. Again, the interval is changing, so this is not an evenly spaced set.
   e. **Evenly spaced:** No matter what y is, this will be an evenly spaced set. For example, if $y=5$, then $2y=10$, which is a difference of 5. Then $3y=15$ and $4y=20$, which is also a difference of 5. Even if y is set equal to zero or one, the result would still be considered evenly spaced (the difference between every term would be the same, namely zero or one).

2. **58:** While you could easily add these up, let's try using the properties of evenly spaced sets. The average/median is going to be $\dfrac{\text{first term + last term}}{2}$, or $\dfrac{13+16}{2}$. This equals $\dfrac{29}{2}$, or 14.5. We now have to multiply this by the number of terms. $4 \times 14.5 = 58$.

3. **40:** While you could plug 3 in for x everywhere, why waste the time? As soon as you notice that this is an evenly spaced set, you know the middle term is the average, and all you need to do is multiply by the number of terms in the set. $2x+2=8$, and $8 \times 5 = 40$.

4. **9,000:** $10,001 - 1,002 + 1 = 9,000$.

5. **8:** Remember that the words "inclusive" and "exclusive" tell you whether or not to include the extremes. In this case, we won't be including either 55 or 144 (though 144 isn't actually a multiple of 11, so doesn't end up mattering). We can solve either through counting or the equation.

   Counting: 66, 77, 88, 99, 110, 121, 132, 143 = 8 terms.
   Equation: $143 - 66 = 77$, $\dfrac{77}{11} = 7$, $7 + 1 = 8$ terms

Problem Set

Solve these problems using the rules for consecutive integers.

1.   How many primes are there from 10 to 41, inclusive?

2.   Will the average of 6 consecutive integers be an integer?

3.   If the sum of a set of 10 consecutive integers is 195, what is the average of the set?

4.   How many terms are there in the set of consecutive integers from -18 to 33, inclusive?

5.

Set A is comprised of all the even numbers between 0 and 20, inclusive.

Quantity A	**Quantity B**
The sum of all the numbers in Set A	150

6.

Quantity A	**Quantity B**
The number of multiples of 7 between 50 and 100, inclusive	The number of multiples of 9 between 30 and 90, inclusive

7.

Set A is comprised of the following terms:
$(3x)$, $(3x - 4)$, $(3x - 8)$, $(3x - 12)$, $(3x - 16)$,
and $(3x - 20)$

Quantity A	**Quantity B**
The sum of all the terms in Set A	$18x - 70$

1. **9:** The primes from 10 to 41, inclusive, are: 11, 13, 17, 19, 23, 29, 31, 37, and 41. Note that the primes are NOT evenly spaced, so you have to list them and count them manually.

2. **NO:** For any set of consecutive integers with an EVEN number of items, the sum of all the items is NEVER a multiple of the number of items. For example, if we pick 4, 5, 6, 7, 8, and 9:

$$\frac{4+5+6+7+8+9}{6} = \frac{39}{6} = 6.5$$

3. **19.5:** Average $= \dfrac{\text{Sum}}{\text{\# of terms}}$. In this problem, we have $\dfrac{195}{10} = 19.5$ as the average.

4. **52:** $33 - (-18) = 51$. Then add one before you are done: $51 + 1 = 52$.

5. **B:** There are two ways to do this question. First, try to estimate the sum. Notice that there will be 11 terms in Set A, and one of them is 0. Even if every term in the set were 20, the sum would only be 220 ($11 \times 20 = 220$). But half of the terms are less than 10. It is unlikely that Quantity A will be bigger than 150.

To do it mathematically, use the equation for the sum of an evenly spaced set. We can find the median by adding up the first and last terms and dividing by two:

$$\frac{0+20}{2} = 10$$

We can then find the number of terms by subtracting the first term from the last term, dividing by the interval (in this case, 2) and adding one. $\dfrac{20-0}{2} = 10$, and $10 + 1 = 11$ terms.

Finally, the sum of the terms will be the average value of the terms (10) times the number of terms (11).

$10 \times 11 = 110$.

Set A is comprised of all the even numbers
between 0 and 20, inclusive.

Quantity A	**Quantity B**
The sum of all the numbers in Set A = 110	150

Therefore **Quantity B is larger.**

6. **C:** Both quantities can be solved straightforwardly with our equations. The first multiple of 7 between 50 and 100 is 56, and the last is 98. $98 - 56 = 42$. $\dfrac{42}{7} = 6$, and $6 + 1 = 7$.

Another way to think about it is that 56 is the 8th multiple of 7, and 98 is the 14th multiple of 7. Now use the counting principle.

$$14 - 8 = 6 + 1 = 7$$

There are 7 multiples of 7 between 50 and 100.

Similarly, the first multiple of 9 between 30 and 90 is 36, and the last is 90. $90 - 36 = 54$. $\dfrac{54}{9} = 6$, and $6 + 1 = 7$.

36 is the 4th multiple of 9, and 90 is the 10th multiple of 9.

$$10 - 4 = 6 + 1 = 7$$

There are 7 multiples of 9 between 30 and 90.

Quantity A	**Quantity B**
The number of multiples of 7 between 50 and 100, inclusive $= 7$	The number of multiples of 9 between 30 and 90, inclusive $= 7$

Therefore **the two quantities are equal.**

7. **A:** The key here is to notice that Set A is an evenly spaced set, and thus we can easily solve for its sum. The median will be equal to $\dfrac{\text{first term} + \text{last term}}{2}$..

$$\frac{(3x) + (3x - 20)}{2} = \frac{6x - 20}{2} = 3x - 10$$

Although there is a formula to figure out how many terms there are, it is easiest in this case to count. There are 6 terms in the set.

The sum of the terms in the set is the average value of the terms $(3x - 10)$ times the number of terms (6).

$$(3x - 10) \times (6) = 18x - 60$$

Rewrite the quantities.

Set A is comprised of the following terms:
$(3x)$, $(3x - 4)$, $(3x - 8)$, $(3x - 12)$, $(3x - 16)$, and $(3x - 20)$

Quantity A	**Quantity B**
$18x - 60$	$18x - 70$

Be careful. Quantity A is subtracting a smaller number (60) than is Quantity B (70), and so has a larger value. **Quantity A is larger.**

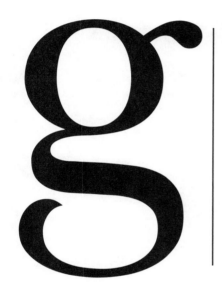

Chapter 8
of
NUMBER PROPERTIES

NUMBER LINES

In This Chapter . . .

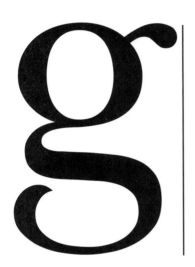

- Relative Position & Relative Distance
- Line Segments

NUMBER LINES

Number lines can appear in a variety of different forms on the GRE. They also provide varying amounts of information.

The most structured version of a number line will contain evenly spaced tick marks. These provide the most detail about the position of points on a number line and about the distance between points.

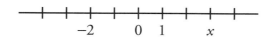

These number lines will almost always contain numbers, and will often contain variables as well. Also note that the distance between tick marks can be an integer amount (like in the number line pictured above) or a fractional amount (like in the number line pictured below).

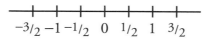

Not all number lines will provide this level of detail. Many number lines will only display a handful of points that are not evenly spaced.

These number lines are likely to contain fewer actual numbers, and will always contain at least one variable. On these number lines, it is more likely that you won't have specific information about the distance between two points.

Additionally, questions that talk about line segments or points that all lie on a line can be thought of as number lines. For example, a question might state that point X is the midpoint of line segment ST. This is the picture you would draw.

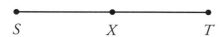

These number lines will rarely contain any real numbers. Often, the only points on the line will be designated by variables. Questions that require this type of number line may or may not provide information about the specific distance between points, although they may provide proportional information. For instance, in the number line above, although we don't know the length of line segment ST, we do know that ST is twice as long as segments SX and XT (because X is the midpoint of ST).

Relative Position & Relative Distance

Questions that involve number lines overwhelmingly ask for information about the *position* of a point or points or the *distance* between two points.

Position

On any number line you will see, numbers get bigger as they move from left to right.

| B is greater than A | B is more positive than A (if both positive) |
| A is less than B | A is more negative than B (if both negative) |

The above statements are true regardless of where zero is shown on the number line. *A* and *B* could both be positive or both be negative, or *A* could be negative and *B* could be positive.

Number lines on the GRE follow rules similar to the rules for geometric shapes. If there is more than one point on a number line, you KNOW the *Relative Position* of each point.

$$A < B < C$$

While you do know the relative position of each point, you DO NOT KNOW the *Relative Distance* between points (unless that information is specifically provided).

On the number line above, *B* could be closer to *A* than to *C*, closer to *C* than to *A*, or equidistant between *A* and *C*. Without more information, there is no way to know.

The rules are similar if a number line contains both numbers and variables.

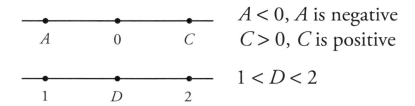

$A < 0$, A is negative
$C > 0$, C is positive

$1 < D < 2$

D looks like it is halfway between 1 and 2, but that does not mean that it is 1.5. *D* could be 1.5, but it could also be 1.000001, or 1.99999 or, in fact, any number between 1 and 2.

Check Your Skills

Refer to the following number line for questions 1–3.

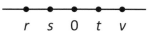

Which of the following MUST be true?

1. $v > s + t$
2. $v + s > t + r$
3. $rs > v$

Answers can be found on page 133.

Distance

If you know the specific location of two points on a number line, the distance between them is the absolute value of their difference.

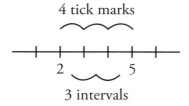

$$\text{Distance} = |8 - (-3)| = |(-3) - 8| = 11$$

If a number line contains tick marks and specifically tells you they are evenly spaced, it may be necessary to calculate the distance between tick marks.

On an evenly spaced number line, tick marks represent specific values, and the intervals between tick marks represent the distance between tick marks.

For any specific range, there will always be 1 more tick mark than interval.

4 tick marks

2   5

3 intervals

On the number line above, there are 4 ticks marks between 2 and 5 (inclusive). There is one fewer interval than tick marks. There are only 3 intervals between 2 and 5. Now calculate the length of the intervals on this number line. To calculate the distance between any two tick marks (which is the same as the length of the intervals), subtract the lower bound from the upper bound and divide the difference by the number of intervals.

In the number line above, the lower bound is 2, the upper bound is 5, and there are 3 intervals between 2 and 5. Use these numbers to calculate the distance between tick marks on the number line.

$$\frac{\text{upper} - \text{lower}}{\# \text{ of intervals}} = \frac{5 - 2}{3} = 1$$

That means that each tick mark in the number line above is 1 unit away from each of the two tick marks to which it is adjacent.

Not every number line will have interval lengths with integer values. Note that this method is equally effective if the intervals are fractional amounts. What is the distance between adjacent tick marks on the following number line?

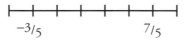

$-3/5$ $7/5$

Now the range contains 6 tick marks and 5 intervals.

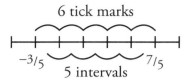

$$\frac{\text{upper} - \text{lower}}{\text{\# of intervals}} = \frac{\frac{7}{5} - \left(-\frac{3}{5}\right)}{3} = \frac{\frac{10}{5}}{5} = \frac{10}{25} = \frac{2}{5}$$

The distance between tick marks is $\frac{2}{5}$.

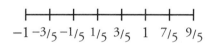

Check Your Skills

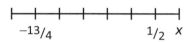

4. On the number line above, what is the value of point *x*?

The answer can be found on page 133.

Line Segments

Some questions on the GRE will describe either several points that all lie on a line or line segments that also lie on the same line. In order to answer these questions correctly, you will need to use the information in the question to construct a number line. Ultimately, position and distance will be of prime importance.

Position

In order to correctly draw number lines, you need to remember one thing. If a question mentions a line segment, there are two possible versions of that segment. Suppose a question tells you that the length of line segment *BD* is 4. These are the two possible versions of *BD*:

We can take this even further. Suppose there are three points on a line: *A*, *B*, and *C*. Without more information, we don't know the order of the three points. Below are some of the possible arrangements:

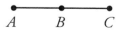 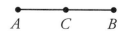 

When questions provide incomplete information about the relative position of points, make sure that you account for the lack of information by drawing multiple number lines.

Distance

Distance on this type of number line can potentially be made more difficult by a lack of complete information about the positions of points on the line.

Suppose that A, B, and C all lie on a number line. Further suppose that $\overline{AB} = 3$ and $\overline{BC} = 7$. Because $\overline{AB}$ is shorter than $\overline{BC}$, there are two possible positions for point A: in between B and C, or on one side of B, with C on the other side.

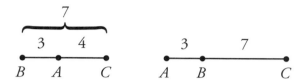

Constructing number lines can be made more difficult by many pieces of information in the question. To construct number lines efficiently and accurately, while remembering to keep track of different possible scenarios, always start with the most restrictive pieces of information first.

> On a line, E is the midpoint of $\overline{DF}$, and $\overline{DE}$ has a length of 6. Point G does not lie on the line and $\overline{EG} = 4$. What is the range of possible values of $\overline{FG}$?

The best way to start this problem is to draw $\overline{DF}$, with E in the middle. There are two possible versions. Also note that $\overline{DE} = 6$.

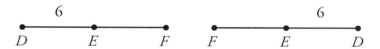

Also, because E is the midpoint of $\overline{DF}$, we know that $\overline{EF}$ also has a length of 6.

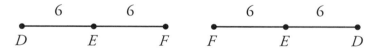

Now we need to deal with point G. Although we do not know the precise position of G, we know it is a fixed distance from E. The set of all points that are equidistant from a fixed point is actually a circle—in other words, to represent the possible positions of G, draw a circle around point E with a radius of 4.

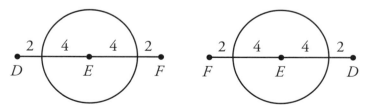

As it turns out, both number lines behave the exact same way, so there is no need to continue to look at both.

On this diagram, you can see that G would be closest to F when it is on the line between E and F. That point is 2 away from F. Similarly, G is farthest away from F when it is on the line between D and E. That point is 10 away from F.

If G could be on the line, the range of possible values of $\overline{FG}$ would be $2 \leq \overline{FG} \leq 10$. Because it can't be on the line, the range is instead $2 < \overline{FG} < 10$.

Check Your Skills

5. X, Y, and Z all lie on a number line. $\overline{XY}$ has a length of 5 and $\overline{YZ}$ has a length of 7. If point U is the midpoint of $\overline{XZ}$, and $\overline{UZ} > 2$, what is the length of $\overline{UZ}$?

The answer can be found on page 133.

Check Your Skills Answer Key:

1. **MUST BE TRUE.** v is already greater than t, and adding a negative number to t will only make it smaller.

2. **MUST BE TRUE.** One way to prove this statement is always true is to add inequalities. We know that $v > t$, and that $s > r$.

$$\begin{array}{r} v > t \\ + s > r \\ \hline v + s > t + r \end{array}$$

3. **NOT ALWAYS TRUE.** v could be any positive number, and r and s could be any negative number.

If $r = -3$, $s = -2$ and $v = 4$, then $rs > v$.

If, however, $r = -2$, $s = -1/2$ and $v = 3$, $v > rs$.

4. $\dfrac{5}{4}$: To find x, we need to figure out how far apart tick marks are. We can use the two given points $(-\dfrac{13}{4}, \dfrac{1}{2})$ to do so. There are five intervals between the two points.

$$\frac{\frac{1}{2} - \left(-\frac{13}{4}\right)}{5} = \frac{\frac{15}{4}}{5} = \frac{15}{20} = \frac{3}{4}$$

If the distance between tick marks is $\dfrac{3}{4}$, then x is $\dfrac{1}{2} + \dfrac{3}{4} = \dfrac{5}{4}$.

5. **6:** Start with the points X, Y, and Z. There are two possible arrangements:

Now place U on each number line.

On one number line, $\overline{UZ} = 1$, but the question stated that $\overline{UZ} > 2$, so $\overline{UZ}$ must equal 6.

Problem Set

For questions 1–6, refer to the number line below. Decide whether each statement MUST be true, COULD be true, or will NEVER be true.

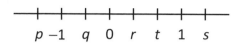

1. $s + q > 0$

2. $pq > t$

3. $p^2 > s^4$

4. $s - p > r - q$

5. $t - q = 2$

6. $rs > 1$

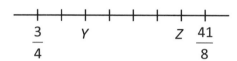

7. If the tick marks on the number line above are evenly spaced, what is the distance between Y and Z?

8. A, B, and C all lie on a line. D is the midpoint of AB and E is the midpoint of BC. $AB = 4$ and $BC = 10$. Which of the following could be the length of AE?

     A) 1   B) 2   C) 3   D) 4   E) 5

9.

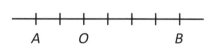

Quantity A	**Quantity B**
$(A)(B)$	-1

10.

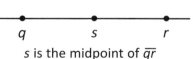

s is the midpoint of $\overline{qr}$

$r = -2q$

Quantity A	**Quantity B**
s	0

11.

A, B, C, and D all lie on a number
line. C is the midpoint of $\overline{AB}$ and D
is the midpoint of $\overline{AC}$.

Quantity A   **Quantity B**

The ratio of $\overline{AD}$ to $\overline{CB}$ The ratio of $\overline{AC}$ to $\overline{AB}$

1. **MUST be true:** Although we don't have specific values for either s or q, we know that s is greater than 1, and we know that q is between 0 and −1. Even if s was as small as it could be (≈ 1.00001) and q was as negative as it could be (≈ -0.99999), the sum would still be positive.

2. **COULD be true:** t must be positive, and the product pq will also be positive. We know that t must be between 0 and 1, but the product pq could be either less than 1 or greater than 1, depending on the numbers chosen. If $t = 0.9$, $q = -0.1$ and $p = -2$, then $t > pq$. However, if $t = 0.5$, $q = -0.9$ and $p = -5$, $pq > t$.

3. **COULD be true:** Both p^2 and s^4 will be positive, but depending on the numbers chosen for p and s, either value could be larger. If $p = -2$ and $s = 3$, $s^4 > p^2$. If $p = -8$ and $s = 2$, $s^4 < p^2$.

4. **MUST be true:** s is greater than 1 and p is less than −1. The smallest that the difference can be is greater than 2.

r must be between 0 and 1 and q must be between 0 and −1. The greatest the difference can be is less than 2. $s - p$ will always be greater than $r - q$.

5. **NEVER be true:** Even if t is as large as it can be and q is as small as it can be, the difference will still have to be less than 2. If $t = 0.999999$ and $q = -0.999999$, $t - q = 1.999998$.

6. **COULD be true:** If $r = 0.1$ and $s = 2$, $rs < 1$. If $r = 0.5$ and $s = 3$, $rs > 1$.

7. **2.5:** To figure out the distance between Y and Z, we first need to figure out the distance between tick marks. We can use the two points on the number line $\left(\dfrac{3}{4} \text{ and } \dfrac{41}{8}\right)$ to find the distance. There are 7 intervals between the two points.

$$\frac{\frac{41}{8} - \frac{3}{4}}{7} = \frac{\frac{41}{8} - \frac{6}{8}}{7} = \frac{\frac{35}{8}}{7} = \frac{5}{8}$$

We actually do not need to know the positions of Y and Z to find the distance between them. We know that there are 4 intervals between Y and Z, so the distance is $4 \times \dfrac{5}{8} = \dfrac{20}{8} = 2.5$.

8. **A:** The trick to this problem is recognizing that there is more than one possible arrangement for the points on the number line. Because $\overline{BC}$ is longer than $\overline{AB}$, A could be either in between B and C or on one side of B with C on the other side of B.

Using the information about the midpoints (D and E) and the lengths of the line segments, we can fill in all the information for our two number lines.

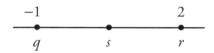

We can see that $\overline{AE}$ has two possible lengths: 1 and 9. 1 is the only option that is an answer choice.

9. **D:** With only one actual number displayed on the number line, we have no way of knowing the distance between tick marks. If the tick marks are a small fractional distance away from each other, then AB will be greater than -1.

For instance, if the distance between tick marks is $\frac{1}{8}$, then A is $-\frac{1}{4}$, B is $\frac{1}{2}$ and AB is $-\frac{1}{8}$, which is greater than -1. If the distance between tick marks is 1, then A is -2, B is 4, and AB is -8, which is less than -1.

Therefore **we do not have enough information** to answer the question.

10. **A:** The easiest approach is to pick numbers. q must be a negative number and r must be positive. If $q = -1$, then $r = 2$.

If s is the midpoint of q and r, then s must be 0.5. Therefore $s > 0$.

For any numbers we pick, s will be positive. Therefore **Quantity A is larger.**

11. **C:**

Visualizing the number line above, the ratio of AD to CB is $\frac{1}{2}$. Similarly, the ratio of AC to AB is $\frac{1}{2}$. Therefore **the two quantities are equal.**

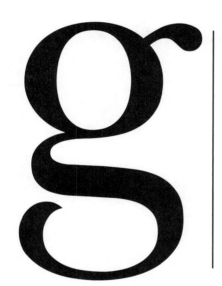

Chapter 9
of
NUMBER PROPERTIES

DRILL SETS

In This Chapter . . .

• Number Properties Drill Sets

Chapter Review: Drill Sets

DRILL SET 1:

Drill 1

1. Is 4,005 divisible by 5?
2. Does 51 have any factors besides 1 and itself?
3. $x = 20$
   The prime factors of x are:
   The factors of x are:

Drill 2

1. Is 123 divisible by 3?
2. Does 23 have any factors besides 1 and itself?
3. $x = 100$
   The prime factors of x are:
   The factors of x are:

Drill 3

1. Is 285,284,901 divisible by 10?
2. Is 539,105 prime?
3. $x = 42$
   The prime factors of x are:
   The factors of x are:

Drill 4

1. Is 9,108 divisible by 9 and/or by 2?
2. Is 937,184 prime?
3. $x = 39$
   The prime factors of x are:
   The factors of x are:

Drill 5

1. Is 43,360 divisible by 5 and/or by 3?
2. Is 81,063 prime?
3. $x = 37$
   The prime factors of x are:
   The factors of x are:

Drill 6: Which of the following are prime numbers?

Determine which of the following numbers are prime numbers. Remember, you only need to find one factor other than the number itself and 1 to prove that the number is not prime.

2	3	5	6
7	9	10	15
17	21	27	29
31	33	258	303
655	786	1,023	1,325

DRILL SET 2:

Drill 1

1. If x is divisible by 33, what other numbers is x divisible by?
2. The prime factorization of a number is $3 \times 3 \times 7$. What is the number and what are all its factors?
3. If x is divisible by 8 and by 3, is x also divisible by 12?

Drill 2

1. If 40 is a factor of x, what other numbers are factors of x?
2. The only prime factors of a number are 5 and 17. What is the number and what are all its factors?
3. 5 and 6 are factors of n. Is n divisible by 15?

Drill 3

1. If 64 divides n, what other divisors does n have?
2. The prime factorization of a number is $2 \times 2 \times 3 \times 11$. What is the number and what are all its factors?
3. 14 and 3 divide n. Is 12 a factor of n?

Drill 4

1. If x is divisible by 4 and by 15, is x a multiple of 18?
2. 91 and 2 go into n. Does 26 divide n?
3. n is divisible by 5 and 12. Is n divisible by 24?

Drill 5

1. If n is a multiple of both 21 and 10, is 30 a divisor of n?
2. 4, 21 and 55 are factors of n. Does 154 divide n?
3. If n is divisible by 196 and by 15, is 210 a factor of n?

DRILL SET 3:

Drill 1: Simplify the following expressions by combining the terms.

1. $x^5 \times x^3 =$
2. $7^6 \times 7^9 =$

3. $3^2 \times 3^5 =$

4. $9^2 \times 9^4 =$

5. $\dfrac{5^5}{5^3} =$

6. $\dfrac{5^3}{5^5} =$

7. $4^{-2} \times 4^5 =$

8. $\dfrac{(-3)^a}{(-3)^2} =$

9. $\dfrac{11^4}{11^x} =$

10. $7^5 \times 5^3 =$

Drill 2: Combine the following expressions.

1. $x^2 \times x^3 \times x^5 =$

2. $3^4 \times 3^2 \times 3 =$

3. $y^3 \times y^{-5} =$

4. $\dfrac{x^5 \times x^6}{x^2} =$

5. $\dfrac{5^6 \times 5^{4x}}{5^4} =$

6. $y^7 \times y^8 \times y^{-6} =$

7. $\dfrac{x^4}{x^{-3}} =$

8. $6^2 \times 6^{-7} \times 6^4 =$

9. $\dfrac{z^5 \times z^{-3}}{z^{-8}} =$

10. $\dfrac{3^{2x} \times 3^{6x}}{3^{-3y}} =$

Drill 3: Simplify the following expressions by combining the terms.

1. $(a^3)^2 =$

2. $(2^2)^4 =$

3. $(3^2)^{-3} =$

4. $(5^2)^x =$

5. $(y^3)^{-4} =$

Drill 4: Combine the following expressions.

1. $(x^2)^6 \times x^3 =$

2. $y^3 \times (y^3)^{-4} =$

3. $\dfrac{(3^5)^2}{3^4} =$

4. $(z^6)^x \times z^{3x} =$

5. $\dfrac{5^3 \times (5^4)^y}{(5^y)^3} =$

Drill 5: Rewrite each negative exponent as a positive exponent.

1. x^{-2}
2. 4^{-4}
3. $y^{-4}z^{-4}$
4. 6^{-3}
5. $x^5 \times x^{-9}$

DRILL SET 4:

Drill 1: Combine the following expressions and solve for x.

1. $x = \sqrt{3} \times \sqrt{27}$

2. $x = \sqrt{2} \times \sqrt{18}$

3. $x = \dfrac{\sqrt{48}}{\sqrt{3}}$

4. $x = \sqrt{5} \times \sqrt{45}$

5. $x = \dfrac{\sqrt{5,000}}{\sqrt{50}}$

Drill 2: Combine the following expressions and solve for x.

1. $x = \sqrt{36} \times \sqrt{4}$

2. $x = \dfrac{\sqrt{128}}{\sqrt{2}}$

3. $x = \dfrac{\sqrt{54} \times \sqrt{3}}{\sqrt{2}}$

4. $x = \dfrac{\sqrt{640}}{\sqrt{2} \times \sqrt{5}}$

5. $x = \dfrac{\sqrt{30}\sqrt{12}}{\sqrt{10}}$

Drill 3: Simplify the following roots.

1. $\sqrt{32}$
2. $\sqrt{24}$

3. $\sqrt{180}$

4. $\sqrt{450}$

5. $\sqrt{490}$

Drill 4: Simplify the following roots.

1. $\sqrt{135}$

2. $\sqrt{224}$

3. $\sqrt{343}$

4. $\sqrt{208}$

5. $\sqrt{432}$

DRILL SET 5:

Drill 1: Simplify the following expressions.

1. $8^3 \times 2^6$
2. $3^4 \times 9^5$
3. $49^2 \times 7^7$
4. $4^3 \times 8^5$
5. $11^8 \times 121^{2x}$

Drill 2: Simplify the following expressions.

1. $25^4 \times 125^3$
2. $9^{-2} \times 27^2$
3. $2^{-7} \times 8^2$
4. $7^{3x} \times 49^{-3}$
5. $4^{5x} \times 32^{-2x}$

Drill 3: Solve the following equations.

1. $x^3 = 27$
2. $y^2 = 81$
3. $2x^3 = 128$
4. $z^2 + 18 = 54$
5. $3x^5 = 96$

Drill 4: Solve the following equations.

1. $3^x = 81$
2. $6^{y-3} = 36$
3. $7^{4x-11} = 7$
4. $5^{-4} = 25^{2x}$
5. $4^2 = 16^{3y-8}$

Drill Set Answers

Set 1, Drill 1

1. Is 4,005 divisible by 5?

   Yes: 4,005 ends in 5, so it is divisible by 5.

2. Does 51 have any factors besides 1 and itself?

   Yes: The digits of 51 add up to a multiple of 3 (5 + 1 = 6), so 3 is a factor of 51. Thus, 51 has factors besides 1 and itself.

3. $x = 20$

   The prime factors of x are:

   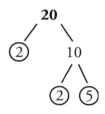

   The factors of x are:

Small	Large
1	20
2	10
4	5

Set 1, Drill 2

1. Is 123 divisible by 3?

   Yes: The digits of 123 add up to a multiple of 3 (1 + 2 + 3 = 6), so 123 is divisible by 3.

2. Does 23 have any factors besides 1 and itself?

   No: 23 is a prime number. It has no factors besides 1 and itself.

3. $x = 100$

   The prime factors of x are:

   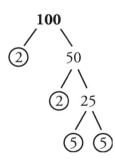

The factors of x are:

Small	Large
1	100
2	50
4	25
5	20
10	10

Set 1, Drill 3

1.   Is 285,284,901 divisible by 10?

No: 285,284,901 ends in a 1, not a 0. It is not divisible by 10.

2.   Is 539,105 prime?

No: 539,105 ends in a 5, so 5 is a factor of 539,105. So are 1 and 539,105. Prime numbers have only two factors, so 539,105 is not prime.

3. $x = 42$

The prime factors of x are:

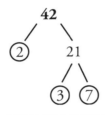

The factors of x are:

Small	Large
1	42
2	21
3	14
6	7

Set 1, Drill 4

1.   Is 9,108 divisible by 9 and/or by 2?

Yes and Yes: The digits of 9,108 add up to a multiple of 9 ($9 + 1 + 0 + 8 = 18$), so it is divisible by 9. 9,108 ends in 8, so it is even, which means it is divisible by 2.

2.   Is 937,184 prime?

No: 937,184 ends in 4, which means it's even. Therefore, it's divisible by 2. It's also divisible by 1 and by 937,184. Prime numbers have only two factors, so 937,184 is not prime.

3. $x = 39$

The prime factors of x are:

The factors of x are:

Small	Large
1	39
3	13

Set 1, Drill 5

1. Is 43,360 divisible by 5 and/or by 3?

   Yes and No: 43,360 ends in 0, so it is divisible by 5. The digits of 43,360 do not add up to a multiple of 3 $(4 + 3 + 3 + 6 + 0 = 16)$ so it is not divisible by 3.

2. Is 81,063 prime?

   No: The digits of 81,063 add up to a multiple of 3 $(8 + 1 + 0 + 6 + 3 = 18)$, so 3 is a factor of 81,063. 1 and 81,063 are also factors of 81,063. Prime numbers have only two factors, so 81,063 is not prime.

3. $x = 37$
   The prime factors of x are: 37
   The factors of x are:

Small	Large
1	37

Set 1, Drill 6: Which of the following are prime numbers?

The numbers in bold below are prime numbers.

2	**3**	**5**	6
7	9	10	15
17	21	27	**29**
31	33	258	303
655	786	1,023	1,325

Prime numbers: 2, 3, 5, 7, 17, 27, 29, 31

Not prime:

All of the even numbers other than 2 (6, 10, 258, 786), since they are divisible by 2.

All of the multiples of 5 (15, 655, 1325).

All of the remaining numbers whose digits add up to a multiple of 3, since they are divisible by 3, by definition: 9 (digits add to 9), 21 (digits add to 2), 33 (digits add to 6), 303 (digits add to 6), 1,023 (digits add to 6). Again, all 5 numbers are divisible by 3.

Set 2, Drill 1

1. If x is divisible by 33, what other numbers is x divisible by?

   If x is divisible by 33, then x is also divisible by everything 33 is divisible by. The factors of 33 are:

Small	Large
1	33
3	11

So x is also divisible by 1, 3 and 11.

2. The prime factorization of a number is $3 \times 3 \times 7$. What is the number and what are all its factors?

$3 \times 3 \times 7 = 63$, which means the number is 63.

Small	Large
1	63
3	21
7	9

3. If x is divisible by 8 and by 3, is x also divisible by 12?

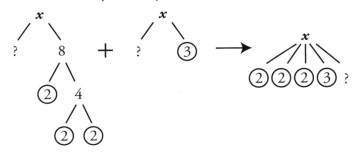

Yes: For x to be divisible by 12, we need to know that it contains the same prime factors as 12. $12 = 2 \times 2 \times 3$. Therefore 12 contains two 2's and a 3. x also contains two 2's and a 3, therefore x is divisible by 12.

Set 2, Drill 2

1. If 40 is a factor of x, what other numbers are factors of x?

If 40 is a factor of x, then any factor of 40 is also a factor of x.

Small	Large
1	40
2	20
4	10
5	8

2. The only prime factors of a number are 5 and 17. What is the number and what are all its factors?

If 5 and 17 are the only prime factors of the number, then the number = 5×17, which means the number is 85.

Small	Large
1	85
5	17

*Manhattan*GRE*Prep
the new standard

3.   5 and 6 are factors of *n*. Is *n* divisible by 15?

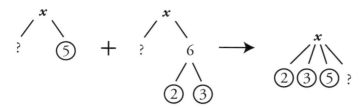

Yes: For *n* to be divisible by 15, we need to know that it contains the same prime factors as 15. 15 = 3 × 5. Therefore 15 contains a 3 and a 5. *n* also contains a 3 and a 5, so *n* is divisible by 15.

Set 2, Drill 3

1.   If 64 divides *n*, what other divisors does *n* have?

If 64 divides *n*, then any divisors of 64 will also be divisors of *n*.

Small	Large
1	64
2	32
4	16
8	8

2.   The prime factorization of a number is 2 × 2 × 3 × 11. What is the number and what are all its factors?

2 × 2 × 3 × 11 = 132

Small	Large
1	132
2	66
3	44
4	33
6	22
11	12

3.   14 and 3 divide *n*. Is 12 a factor of *n*?

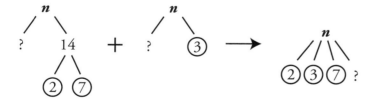

Cannot tell: For 12 to be a factor of *n*, *n* must contain all the same prime factors as 12. 12 = 2 × 2 × 3, so 12 contains two 2s and a 3. *n* also contains a 3 but only contains one 2 that we know of, so we don't know whether 12 is a factor of *n*.

Set 2, Drill 4

1.   If *x* is divisible by 4 and by 15, is *x* a multiple of 18?

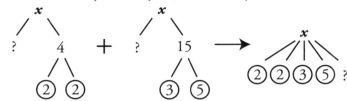

Cannot tell: For *x* to be a multiple of 18, *x* would have to be divisible by 18. For *x* to be divisible by 18, it has to contain all the same prime factors as 18. 18 = 2 × 2 × 3 × 3, so 18 contains two 2's and two 3's. *x* contains two 2's, but it only contains one 3 that we know of, so we don't know whether *x* is a multiple of 18.

2.   91 and 2 go into *n*. Does 26 divide *n*?

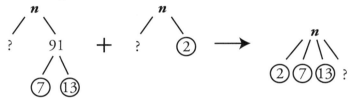

Yes: For 26 to divide *n*, *n* has to contain all the same prime factors as 26. 26 = 2 × 13, so 26 contains a 2 and a 13. *n* also contains a 2 and a 13, so 26 divides *n*.

3.   *n* is divisible by 5 and 12. Is *n* divisible by 24?

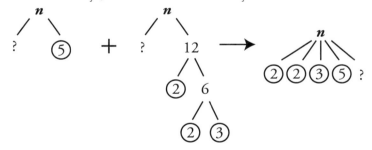

Cannot tell: For *n* to be divisible by 24, it has to contain all the same prime factors as 24. 24 = 2 × 2 × 2 × 3, so 24 contains three 2's and a 3. *n* contains a 3, but only contains two 2's that we know of, so we don't know whether *n* is divisible by 24.

Set 2, Drill 5

1.   If n is a multiple of both 21 and 10, is 30 a divisor of n?

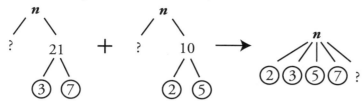

Yes: For 30 to be a divisior of n, n has to contain all the same prime factors that 30 contains. $30 = 2 \times 3 \times 5$, so 30 contains a 2, a 3 and a 5. n also contains a 2, a 3 and a 5, so 30 is a divisor of n.

2.   4, 21 and 55 are factors of n. Does 154 divide n?

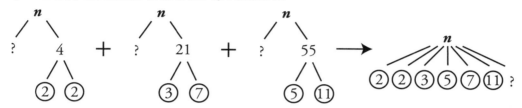

Yes: For 154 to divide n, n has to contain all the same prime factors as 154. $154 = 2 \times 7 \times 11$, so 154 contains a 2, a 7 and an 11. n also contains a 2, a 7 and an 11, so 154 divides n.

3.   If n is divisible by 196 and by 15, is 210 a factor of n?

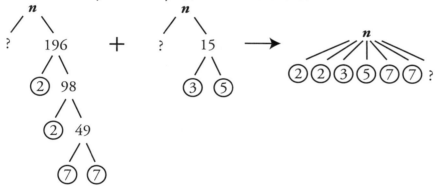

Yes: For 210 to be a factor of n, n must contain all the same prime factors as 210. $210 = 2 \times 3 \times 5 \times 7$, so 210 contains a 2, a 3, a 5 and a 7. n contains a 2, a 3, a 5 and a 7, so 210 is a factor of n.

Set 3, Drill 1:

1. x^8: $x^5 \times x^3 = x^{(5+3)} = x^8$

2. 7^{15}: $7^6 \times 7^9 = 7^{(6+9)} = 7^{15}$

3. 3^7: $3^2 \times 3^5 = 3^{(2+5)} = 3^7$

4. 9^6: $9^2 \times 9^4 = 9^{(2+4)} = 9^6$

5. 5^2: $\dfrac{5^5}{5^3} = 5^{(5-3)} = 5^2$

6. 5^{-2}: $\dfrac{5^3}{5^5} = 5^{(3-5)} = 5^{-2}$

7. 4^3: $4^{-2} \times 4^5 = 4^{(-2+5)} = 4^3$

8. $(-3)^{(a-2)}$: $\dfrac{(-3)^a}{(-3)^2} = (-3)^{(a-2)}$

9. $11^{(4-x)}$: $\dfrac{11^4}{11^x} = 11^{(4-x)}$

10. $7^5 \times 5^3 =$ Can't simplify—no common bases or exponents!

Set 3, Drill 2:

1. x^{10}: $x^2 \times x^3 \times x^5 = x^{(2+3+5)} = x^{10}$
2. 3^7: $3^4 \times 3^2 \times 3 = 3^{(4+2+1)} = 3^7$
3. y^{-2}: $y^3 \times y^{-5} = y^{(3-5)} = y^{-2}$

4. x^9: $\dfrac{x^5 \times x^6}{x^2} = x^{(5+6-2)} = x^9$.

5. 5^{4x+2}: $\dfrac{5^6 \times 5^{4x}}{5^4} = 5^{(6+4x-4)} = 5^{4x+2}$

6. y^9: $y^7 \times y^8 \times y^{-6} = y^{(7+8+(-6))} = y^9$

7. x^7: $\dfrac{x^4}{x^{-3}} = x^{(4-(-3))} = x^7$

8. 6^{-1}: $6^2 \times 6^{-7} \times 6^4 = 6^{(2+(-7)+4)} = 6^{-1}$

9. z^{10}: $\dfrac{z^4 \times z^{-3}}{z^{-8}} = z^{(5+(-3)-(-8))} = z^{10}$

10. 3^{8x+3y}: $\dfrac{3^{2x} \times 3^{6x}}{3^{-3y}} = 3^{(2x+6x-(-3y))} = 3^{8x+3y}$

Set 3, Drill 3:

1. a^6: $(a^3)^2 = a^{(3 \times 2)} = a^6$
2. 2^8: $(2^2)^4 = 2^{(2 \times 4)} = 2^8$
3. 3^{-6}: $(3^2)^{-3} = 3^{(2 \times -3)} = 3^{-6}$
4. 5^{2x}: $(5^2)^x = 5^{(2 \times x)} = 5^{2x}$
5. y^{-12}: $(y^3)^{-4} = y^{(3 \times -4)} = y^{-12}$

Set 3, Drill 4:

1. x^{15}: $(x^2)^6 \times x^3 = x^{(2 \times 6+3)} = x^{(12+3)} = x^{15}$

2. y^{-9}: $y^3 \times (y^3)^{-4} = y^{(3+3 \times -4)} = y^{(3+(-12))} = y^{-9}$

3. 3^6: $\dfrac{(3^5)^2}{3^4} = 3^{(5 \times 2-4)} = 3^{(10-4)} = 3^6$

4. z^{9x}: $(z^6)^x \times z^{3x} = z^{(6 \times x+3x)} = z^{(6x+3x)} = z^{9x}$

5. 5^{y+3}: $\dfrac{5^3 \times (5^4)^y}{(5^y)^3} = 5^{(3+(4 \times y)-(y \times 3))} = 5^{(3+4y-3y)} = 5^{y+3}$

Set 3, Drill 5:

1. $x^{-2} = \dfrac{1}{x^2}$

2. $4^{-4} = \dfrac{1}{4^4} = \dfrac{1}{256}$

3. $y^{-4}z^{-4} = \dfrac{1}{y^4 z^4}$

4. $6^{-3} = \dfrac{1}{6^3} = \dfrac{1}{216}$

5. $x^5 \times x^{-9} = x^{5+(-9)} = x^{-4} = \dfrac{1}{x^4}$

Set 4, Drill 1:

1. **9:** $x = \sqrt{3} \times \sqrt{27} = \sqrt{3 \times 27} = \sqrt{81} = 9$
2. **6:** $x = \sqrt{2} \times \sqrt{18} = \sqrt{2 \times 18} = \sqrt{36} = 6$
3. **4:** $x = \dfrac{\sqrt{48}}{\sqrt{3}} = \sqrt{\dfrac{48}{3}} = \sqrt{16} = 4$
4. **15:** $x = \sqrt{5} \times \sqrt{45} = \sqrt{5 \times 45} = \sqrt{225} = 15$
5. **10:** $x = \dfrac{\sqrt{5,000}}{\sqrt{50}} = \sqrt{\dfrac{5,000}{50}} = \sqrt{100} = 10$

Set 4, Drill 2:

1. **12:** $x = \sqrt{36} \times \sqrt{4} = \sqrt{36 \times 4} = \sqrt{144} = 12$ OR
   $x = \sqrt{36} \times \sqrt{4} = 6 \times 2 = 12$

2. **8:** $x = \dfrac{\sqrt{128}}{\sqrt{2}} = \sqrt{\dfrac{128}{2}} = \sqrt{64} = 8$

3. **9:** $x = \dfrac{\sqrt{54} \times \sqrt{3}}{\sqrt{2}} = \sqrt{\dfrac{54 \times 3}{2}} = \sqrt{81} = 9$

4. **8:** $x = \dfrac{\sqrt{640}}{\sqrt{2} \times \sqrt{5}} = \sqrt{\dfrac{640}{2 \times 5}} = \sqrt{64} = 8$

5. **6:** $x = \dfrac{\sqrt{30}\sqrt{12}}{\sqrt{10}} = \sqrt{\dfrac{30 \times 12}{10}} = \sqrt{36} = 6$

Set 4, Drill 3:

1. $\mathbf{4\sqrt{2}}: \sqrt{32} = \sqrt{2\times2\times2\times2\times2} = \sqrt{2\times2}\times\sqrt{2\times2}\times\sqrt{2} = 2\times2\times\sqrt{2} = 4\sqrt{2}$

2. $\mathbf{2\sqrt{6}}: \sqrt{24} = \sqrt{2\times2\times2\times3} = \sqrt{2\times2}\times\sqrt{2\times3} = 2\sqrt{6}$

3. $\mathbf{6\sqrt{5}}: \sqrt{180} = \sqrt{2\times2\times3\times3\times5} = \sqrt{2\times2}\times\sqrt{3\times3}\times\sqrt{5} = 2\times3\times\sqrt{5} = 6\sqrt{5}$

4. $\mathbf{15\sqrt{2}}: \sqrt{450} = \sqrt{2\times3\times3\times5\times5} = \sqrt{3\times3}\times\sqrt{5\times5}\times\sqrt{2} = 3\times5\times\sqrt{2} = 15\sqrt{2}$

5. $\mathbf{7\sqrt{10}}: \sqrt{490} = \sqrt{2\times5\times7\times7} = \sqrt{7\times7}\times\sqrt{2\times5} = 7\sqrt{10}$

Set 4, Drill 4:

1. $\mathbf{3\sqrt{15}}: \sqrt{135} = \sqrt{3\times3\times3\times5} = \sqrt{3\times3}\times\sqrt{3\times5} = 3\sqrt{15}$

2. $\mathbf{4\sqrt{14}}: \sqrt{224} = \sqrt{2\times2\times2\times2\times2\times7} = \sqrt{2\times2}\times\sqrt{2\times2}\times\sqrt{2\times7} = 2\times2\times\sqrt{14} = 4\sqrt{14}$

3. $\mathbf{7\sqrt{7}}: \sqrt{343} = \sqrt{7\times7\times7} = \sqrt{7\times7}\times\sqrt{7} = 7\sqrt{7}$

4. $\mathbf{4\sqrt{13}}: \sqrt{208} = \sqrt{2\times2\times2\times2\times13} = \sqrt{2\times2}\times\sqrt{2\times2}\times\sqrt{13} = 2\times2\times\sqrt{13} = 4\sqrt{13}$

5. $\mathbf{12\sqrt{3}}: \sqrt{432} = \sqrt{2\times2\times2\times2\times3\times3\times3} = \sqrt{2\times2}\times\sqrt{2\times2}\times\sqrt{3\times3}\times\sqrt{3} = 2\times2\times3\times\sqrt{3} = 12\sqrt{3}$

Set 5, Drill 1:

1. $\mathbf{2^{15}}: 8^3 \times 2^6 = (2^3)^3 \times 2^6 = 2^9 \times 2^6 = 2^{15}$

2. $\mathbf{3^{14}}: 3^4 \times 9^5 = 3^4 \times (3^2)^5 = 3^4 \times 3^{10} = 3^{14}$

3. $\mathbf{7^{11}}: 49^2 \times 7^7 = (7^2)^2 \times 7^7 = 7^4 \times 7^7 = 7^{11}$

4. $\mathbf{2^{21}}: 4^3 \times 8^5 = (2^2)^3 \times (2^3)^5 = 2^6 \times 2^{15} = 2^{21}$

5. $\mathbf{11^{4x+8}}: 11^8 \times 121^{2x} = 11^8 \times (11^2)^{2x} = 11^8 \times 11^{4x} = 11^{4x+8}$

Set 5, Drill 2:

1. $\mathbf{5^{17}}: 25^4 \times 125^3 = (5^2)^4 \times (5^3)^3 = 5^8 \times 5^9 = 5^{17}$

2. $\mathbf{3^2}: 9^{-2} \times 27^2 = (3^2)^{-2} \times (3^3)^2 = 3^{-4} \times 3^6 = 3^2$

3. $\mathbf{2^{-1}}: 2^{-7} \times 8^2 = 2^{-7} \times (2^3)^2 = 2^{-7} \times 2^6 = 2^{-1}$

4. $\mathbf{7^{3x-6}}: 7^{3x} \times 49^{-3} = 7^{3x} \times (7^2)^{-3} = 7^{3x} \times 7^{-6} = 7^{3x-6}$

5. $\mathbf{1}: 4^{5x} \times 32^{-2x} = (2^2)^{5x} \times (2^5)^{-2x} = 2^{10x} \times 2^{-10x} = 2^0 = 1$

Set 5, Drill 3:

1. $x^3 = 27$
   $x = \mathbf{3}$

2. $y^2 = 81$
   $y = \mathbf{9 \ OR\ {-9}}$

3. $2x^3 = 128$
   $x^3 = 64$
   $x = \mathbf{4}$

4. $z^2 + 18 = 54$
   $z^2 = 36$
   $z = \mathbf{6\ OR\ {-6}}$

5. $3x^5 = 96$
   $x^5 = 32$
   $x = \mathbf{2}$

Set 5, Drill 4:

1.   **4:** $3^x = 81$
   $3^x = 3^4$
   $x = 4$

2.   **5:** $6^{y-3} = 36$
   $6^{y-3} = 6^2$
   $y - 3 = 2$
   $y = 5$

3.   **3:** $7^{4x-11} = 7^1$
   $4x - 11 = 1$
   $4x = 12$
   $x = 3$

4.   **−1:** $5^{-4} = 25^{2x}$
   $5^{-4} = (5^2)^{2x}$
   $5^{-4} = 5^{4x}$
   $-4 = 4x$
   $-1 = x$

5.   **3:** $4^2 = 16^{3y-8}$
   $4^2 = (4^2)^{3y-8}$
   $4^2 = 4^{6y-16}$
   $2 = 6y - 16$
   $18 = 6y$
   $3 = y$

OR

$$(2^2) = ((2^2)^2)^{3y-8}$$
$$(2^2)^2 = (2^4)^{3y-8}$$
$$2^4 = 2^{12y-32}$$
$$4 = 12y - 32$$
$$2 = 6y - 16$$
$$18 = 6y$$
$$3 = y$$

OR

$$4^2 = 16^{3y-8}$$
$$16 = 16^{3y-8}$$
$$16^1 = 16^{3y-8}$$
$$1 = 3y - 8$$
$$9 = 3y$$
$$3 = y$$

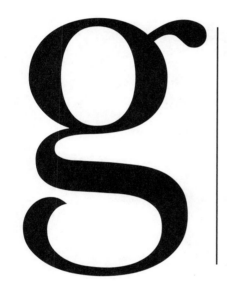

Chapter 10

of

NUMBER PROPERTIES

NUMBER PROPERTIES PRACTICE QUESTION SETS

In This Chapter . . .

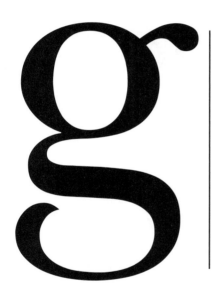

Number Properties: Easy Practice Question Set

1. If ab is positive and cde is negative, which of the following *must* be true?

(A) $ab + cde > 0$

(B) $ab \times cde \times cde > 0$

(C) $ac + de < 0$

(D) $\dfrac{ab}{cde} < -1$

(E) $\dfrac{a}{cde} < 0$

2. If x, y, and z are integers, and x and y are both even, which of the following *could* be an odd integer?

(A) $y + x$

(B) $xy + y$

(C) $y - xz$

(D) $x + yz$

(E) $xy + z$

3. John drives 6 miles roundtrip to work every weekday. On Saturday, John drives 2 miles roundtrip to the grocery store and 6 miles roundtrip to a nearby lake. John does not drive anywhere else.

Quantity A	**Quantity B**
The number of miles John drives in a week	The highest odd number less than 40

4. Simplify the expression $\sqrt{x^2 + x^2(3)}$.

(A) x

(B) $2x$

(C) $x + 3x$

(D) $x + x\sqrt{3}$

(E) $x\sqrt{2}$

5. There are 37 adults participating in a dance class, with an odd number of men and an even number of women. If male and female dance partners are paired up, there will be 3 women left out. How many men are in the class?

☐

6.

$$b - c + a > b + c + a \text{ and } c - b - a < c + b - a$$

Quantity A	**Quantity B**
b	c

7. If x is a positive integer and y is a negative integer, which of the following *cannot* be negative?

    (A) $x + y$
    (B) $2x + y$
    (C) $x + 2y$
    (D) $2y$
    (E) $2x - y$

8.

The set S consists of 4 consecutive integers. The second term in the set is n.

Quantity A	**Quantity B**
The average value of the integers in set S	$n + \dfrac{1}{2}$

9. Suppose that $(-3)^3x = (-3)^6y^2$ and that $y \neq 0$. Which of the following *must* be true? Indicate *all* that apply.

    [A] x is always negative
    [B] x is negative only if y is negative
    [C] x is positive only if y is negative

10.

x is an integer and $x > 1$

Quantity A	**Quantity B**
$\sqrt{(32)(2)(x^2) + (12)(3)(x^2)}$	20

11.

Let S be the sum of the elements of X, a set of 10 consecutive positive integers.

Quantity A	**Quantity B**
$\dfrac{S}{10} - 5$	The smallest of the integers in X

12. If $x = 2$, the value of $(x^2)^3 + x$ is

    (A) 32
    (B) 34
    (C) 64
    (D) 66
    (E) 128

13.

On the number line, p is to the right of q and is to the left of r.

Quantity A	**Quantity B**
$p - q$	$p - r$

14. If the sum of seven consecutive integers is zero, what is the smallest of the seven integers?

(A) -6
(B) -3
(C) -2
(D) 0
(E) 6

15. Which of the following is the product of an even prime number and an odd prime number?

(A) 4
(B) 6
(C) 8
(D) 12
(E) 18

16.

Quantity A	**Quantity B**
$(-2 + 3)(2 - (-3))$	$(-3 + 2)(3 - (-2))$

17.

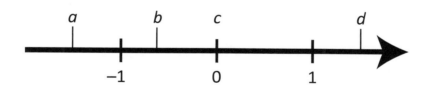

Which <u>two</u> of the numbers labeled on the number line above will have a product that is positive?

[A] a
[B] b
[C] c
[D] d

18. What is a non-zero solution to the equation $2x^5 - 30x^4 = 0$?

[ ]

19.

Quantity A	**Quantity B**
$(4^2)^3 - 4^3$	$(4^3)^2 - 4^2$

20.

$$a = 140 \text{ and } b = 33$$

Quantity A	**Quantity B**
The largest prime factor of a	The largest prime factor of b

Number Properties: Medium Practice Question Set

1. A number line is divided by 10 evenly spaced tick marks. The length between each tick mark equals p, and p is a prime number.

Indicate _all_ the possible lengths of the number line described above:

A	10
B	18
C	22
D	24
E	27
F	30
G	36
H	117
I	130

2.

$$\frac{x}{100} \text{ is an integer.}$$

Quantity A	**Quantity B**
x^3	$x^2 + 100$

3. Let X represent a number line such that $-1 < x < 5$. Let Y represent a number line such that $6 \leq y \leq 10$. If X were shifted by 5 in the positive direction and Y were shifted by 2 in the positive direction, how many common integers would the new X and in the new Y share?

    (A) 1
    (B) 2
    (C) 3
    (D) 4
    (E) 5

4.

Quantity A	**Quantity B**
$(7^{21} + 7^{-21})^2$	$7^{42} + 7^{-42}$

5. If $|a + b| - c < d$, which of the following _must_ be true?
Indicate _all_ that apply.

A	$a + b > 0$
B	$d > 0$ whenever $c < 0$
C	$d + c > 0$

6. Which of the following is equal to $\sqrt{81+169}$?

   (A) $5\sqrt{10}$
   (B) 22
   (C) 25
   (D) $25\sqrt{2}$
   (E) $25\sqrt{5}$

7. How many multiples of 11 are there between 100 and 1,000, inclusive?

   (A) 80
   (B) 81
   (C) 82
   (D) $\dfrac{900}{11}$
   (E) 901

8. Suppose each integer in the line segment $5 < x < 10$ is divided into thirds with a dark gray tick mark at each third $\left(\dfrac{1}{3}\right)$, and each integer is divided into ninths with a light gray line at each ninth $\left(\dfrac{1}{9}\right)$. At how many places will a dark gray tick mark and a light gray line overlap?

9. Suppose that $|b - a| = 2$. Which of the following statements must be true?

Indicate _all_ that apply.

   [A] a must be positive if b is positive
   [B] a must be negative if b is negative
   [C] $b > 0$ if $a > 2$

10. x, y, r, and t are integers such that x^y is negative and r^t is positive. If t is <u>not</u> a multiple of 2, then which of the following statements <u>must</u> be true?

   (A) $xr > 0$
   (B) $x - r < 0$
   (C) y is a multiple of 2
   (D) $x^t > 0$
   (E) None of the above

11.

Quantity A	**Quantity B**
$\dfrac{(3^3)^2 (15)^3}{5^3}$	3^8

12. If p and q are different prime numbers and a, b, and c are consecutive integers such that $a < b < c$, which of the following must be odd?

    (A) ap
    (B) bp
    (C) pq
    (D) $a + b$
    (E) $a + q$

13.

Quantity A	**Quantity B**
$\sqrt{20} + \sqrt{80}$	10

14.

$$a > b \text{ and } |b| > |a|$$

Quantity A	**Quantity B**
ab^2	$a^2 b$

15. If q is an even integer and r is an odd integer, then which of the following MUST be an even integer?

    (A) $q + r$
    (B) $q^2 + r$
    (C) $q + r^2$
    (D) $qr + q$
    (E) $qr + r$

16.

$$m \text{ is the product of two positive even integers.}$$

Quantity A	**Quantity B**
The last digit of $\dfrac{m}{4}$	5

17. If $u < v < 0 < w$, then which of the following _must_ be positive?

    (A) $w - uv$
    (B) $u - wv$
    (C) $u(w - v)$
    (D) $v(u - w)$
    (E) $w(u - v)$

*Manhattan*GRE*Prep

18. Points *X*, *Y*, *Z* and *W* lie on a number line, though not necessarily in that order. The distance between *X* and *Y* is 10; the distance between *Z* and *W* is 7; and the distance between *Y* and *Z* is 4. What is the minimum possible distance between *X* and *W*?

   (A) 1
   (B) 3
   (C) 4
   (D) 6
   (E) 7

19. If $a \neq 0$, which of the following is equivalent to $\dfrac{a(a^2)^{-1}}{a^{-1}}$?

   (A) a^{-3}
   (B) a^{-2}
   (C) a^{-1}
   (D) a^0
   (E) a^1

20.

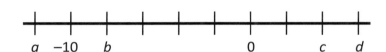

On the number line above, all tick marks are evenly spaced.

Quantity A	**Quantity B**
ac	*bd*

Manhattan GRE® Prep
the new standard

Number Properties: Hard Practice Question Set

CAUTION: These problems are *very difficult*—more difficult than many of the problems you will likely see on the GRE. Consider these "Challenge Problems." Have fun!

1. If a is a positive integer, then which of the following must be true of $(a-1)(a)(a+1)$?
    Indicate _all_ that apply.

    A It is always positive.
    B It is always odd.
    C It is always divisible by 3.
    D It is always divisible by 4.
    E It is non-prime.

2.

Quantity A	**Quantity B**
$\dfrac{6^8 5^3 4^2}{3^6 8^2}$	$\dfrac{6^9 5^3 4^3}{3^8 2^8}$

3. If $3^{2a}11^b = 27^{4x}33^{2x}$, then x _must_ equal which of the following?
    Indicate _all_ that apply.

    A $2a$
    B $2b$
    C $7a - 2b$
    D $\dfrac{a}{7}$
    E $\dfrac{b}{2}$

4. Suppose that $|x| < |y+2| < |z|$. Suppose further that $y > 0$ and that $xz > 0$. Which of the following *could* be true?
    Indicate _all_ statements that apply.

    A $0 < y < x < z$
    B $0 < x < y < z$
    C $x < z < 0 < y$
    D $0 < y + 1.5 < x < z$
    E $z < x < 0 < y$

5. Suppose that M and N are positive 2-digit integers and that $N = \dfrac{M+5}{2}$. If $\dfrac{M}{3}$ is _not_ an integer, what is the largest possible value of N?

6. What is the smallest positive integer that is non-prime and is _not_ a factor of 11!?

7. If x and y are integers, then $\dfrac{(x)(x+1)(x+2)}{2\times 3\times 5^{y}}$ _must_ be an integer if which of the following is true?

    (A) x is even
    (B) x is odd
    (C) x is divisible by three
    (D) y is even
    (E) y is equal to zero

8. If ab is divisible by c, which of the following _cannot_ be true?

    (A) a is divisible by c
    (B) a is not divisible by c
    (C) c is a prime number
    (D) $ab + c$ is odd and c is odd
    (E) $ab + c$ is odd and c is even

9. If $\dfrac{x^{2}}{4}$ is an integer greater than 50, then what is the smallest possible value for x^2?

10. Which of the following equals $-(\sqrt{2}-\sqrt{8})(2\sqrt{2}+\sqrt{8})$?

    (A) $-8\sqrt{2}$
    (B) -4
    (C) 4
    (D) $4\sqrt{2}$
    (E) 8

11. m is a positive integer less than 300 and has exactly two even and two odd prime factors in its prime factorization. What is the maximum possible value of m?

12.

$$xy < 0$$

Quantity A   **Quantity B**

$|x+y|$ $|x| + |y|$

13. The quantity $3^3 4^4 5^5 6^6 - 3^6 4^5 5^4 6^3$ will end in how many zeros?

    (A) 3
    (B) 4
    (C) 5
    (D) 6
    (E) 9

14.

x is a positive, odd integer.

Quantity A	**Quantity B**
$(-3)^x$	-2^{2x}

15.

Quantity A	**Quantity B**
$\dfrac{3^{20} - 3^{19}}{3}$	$3^{18} + 3^{18}$

16. x, y and z are consecutive integers, where $x < y < z$. Which of the following _must_ be divisible by 3?

Indicate _all_ that apply.

    [A] xyz
    [B] $(x + 1)yz$
    [C] $(x + 2)yz$
    [D] $(x + 3)yz$
    [E] $(x + 1)(y + 1)(z + 1)$
    [F] $(x + 1)(y + 2)(z + 3)$

17. b, c, and d are consecutive even integers such that $2 < b < c < d$. What is the largest positive integer that _must_ be a divisor of bcd?

18. x^2 is divisible by both 40 and 75. If x has _exactly_ 3 distinct prime factors, which of the following could be the value of x?

Indicate _all_ values that apply.

    [A] 30
    [B] 60
    [C] 200
    [D] 240
    [E] 420

19. m is a three-digit integer such that when it is divided by 5, the remainder is y, and when it is divided by 7, the remainder is also y. If y is a positive integer, what is the smallest possible value of m?

20.

$$x = 120 \text{ and } y = 150$$

Quantity A	**Quantity B**
The number of positive divisors of x	The number of positive divisors of y

Number Properties: Easy Practice Question Solutions

1. **B:** One approach to this problem is to pick numbers.

However, this could lead to mistakes, or to multiple answer choices that seemingly lead to a correct answer. Since the Choices largely concern the sign of various expressions, one could work with the signs of the variables. In either case, all positive/negative scenarios must be considered.

For instance, *a* and *b* can be either *both* positive or *both* negative. Similarly, *cde* must have either *one* or *three* negative variables. Choice B _must_ be positive because the first term, *ab*, is positive; the second term, *cde*, is negative, and the third term, *cde*, is also negative. Positive × negative × negative = positive.

Choices A, C, and E can be proven to be either positive or negative by testing the various combinations of signed numbers for all the variables in the expressions. Finally, since nothing is known of the magnitude of the values of the variables, Choice D could be either true or false. Either *ab* or *cde* could have a greater absolute value. Note that Choice D _must_ be negative (even though it could be between 0 and −1).

2. **E:** The product of two even numbers, such as *xy*, will always be even. However, *z* _could_ be odd, and an even plus an odd is always odd. Therefore the expression in Choice E could be odd.

In Choices A and B, an even plus an even must be even. In Choice C, an even minus an even must be even. In Choice D, *yz* (an even number, because *y* is even) plus *x*, which is even, will be even.

Note that this problem could be easily solved by either applying these odd/even principles as demonstrated, or by picking numbers for *x*, *y*, and *z*.

3. **B:** John drives 6 miles on each of the 5 weekdays for a total of 30 miles. He drives an additional 8 miles on Saturday for a total of 38 miles. The highest odd number less than 40 is 39. The comparison simplifies to:

38	39

Therefore **Quantity B is greater.**

4. **B:** $\sqrt{x^2 + x^2(3)} = \sqrt{4x^2} = 2x$. Note that we _cannot_ split expressions under the radical. In other words, splitting $\sqrt{x^2 + x^2(3)}$ into $\sqrt{x^2} + \sqrt{x^2(3)}$ is _incorrect_, and will lead to the incorrect answer (in this case, Choice D).

5. **17:** Since there are 3 women left out, there will be $37 - 3 = 34$ people dancing in pairs. Half of those dancing are men; hence there are 17 men in the class. This is partially verified by the fact that 17 is an odd number.

6. **A:** The first inequality simplifies to:

$$b - c + a > b + c + a$$
$$-c + a > c + a$$
$$-c > c$$
$$0 > 2c$$
$$c < 0$$

The second inequality simplifies to:

$$c - b - a < c + b - a$$
$$-b - a < b - a$$
$$-b < b$$
$$0 < 2b$$
$$b > 0$$

Since b is positive and c is negative, b must be larger. Therefore **Quantity A is greater.**

7. **E:** Suppose y is a large negative number and x is a small positive number. In that case, $x + y$, $2x + y$, and $x + 2y$ would all yield a negative number. Because y is negative, $2y$ will be negative. In Choice E, $2x$ will be positive, y will be negative, and a positive minus a negative will always yield a positive.

8. **C:** Given the fact that the integers in set S are consecutive and the value of the second term is n, the remaining terms can be expressed as $n - 1$, $n + 1$, and $n + 2$, with $n - 1$ the first term in the sequence.

The average of a set of numbers can be expressed as (Sum) ÷ (Number of Terms), which for this problem equals:

$$\frac{(n-1) + n + (n+1) + (n+2)}{4} = \frac{4n+2}{4} = n + \frac{1}{2}.$$

Therefore, **the two quantities are equal.**

9. **A:** Notice that $(-3)^3$ is negative while $(-3)^6$ and y^2 are both positive (*this is a property of any number, with the exception of zero, raised to an even power*). We can therefore rewrite the original equation as: $(\text{Neg})x = (\text{Pos})(\text{Pos})$.

It is clear from the answer choices that the question involves only the sign of x. Given our new equation, it is clear that x must be negative in order for the equation to hold—thus only Choice A is correct.

10. **D:** We begin by simplifying the value in Quantity A. Because of order of operations, we must first perform the multiplication, then addition, and finally the square-root—we cannot separate the expression under the radical. This gives $\sqrt{64x^2 + 36x^2} = \sqrt{100x^2} = 10x$. Since x must be a positive integer larger than 1, Quantity A must be 20 or larger. Thus the comparison becomes:

≥ 20 20

Thus if $x = 2$, the two quantities are equal; otherwise, Quantity A is larger. **We do not have enough information** to decide which is the case.

11. **B:** If the sum of 10 consecutive positive integers is S, then the average value in the set is $\frac{S}{10}$. This number can also be found by averaging the 5th and 6th numbers in the set (ie—finding the "middle" value), which is exactly 4.5 greater than the lowest number. (For example, the set {1, 2, 3, 4, 5, 6, 7, 8, 9, 10} has a sum $S = 55$. The average value is $\frac{S}{10} = 5.5$, which is halfway between the numbers 5 and 6. Thus, this number is exactly 4.5 higher than the smallest number in the set, which is 1.)

*Manhattan*GRE*Prep
the new standard

Using this logic, we may write the smallest number in the set as $\frac{S}{10} - 4.5$. The comparison then becomes:

$$\frac{S}{10} - 5 \qquad\qquad\qquad\qquad \frac{S}{10} - 4.5$$

Therefore **Quantity B is larger.**

12. **D**: To solve this problem, we need to apply the appropriate exponent rule: $(x^a)^b = x^{ab}$. Thus, $(2^2)^3 + 2 = 2^6 + 2 = 64 + 2 = 66$.

13. **A:** If p is to the right of q on the number line, then $p > q$. Similarly, if p is to the left of r on the number line, then $p < r$. Therefore $p - q > 0$ and $p - r < 0$. Thus, **Quantity A is greater.**

14. **B:** If the sum of an evenly spaced set is zero, then zero is the average number in the set; the average is equal to the median or "middle" number, so the middle number is zero. Since there are seven terms and they are separated by increments of one, the set must be: $\{-3, -2, -1, 0, 1, 2, 3\}$. Thus the smallest integer in the set is -3.

15. **B:** The only even prime number is 2. The first few odd prime numbers are 3, 5, 7 and 11. Looking through the Choices, we can see that Choice B (6) is the only one that is the product of 2 and an odd prime (2×3). Note that Choice E (18) fails, because $18 = 2 \times 9$, and 9 is odd but non-prime.

16. **A:** You may be tempted to use the calculator for this problem, but the solution is much easier and much quicker without it. When a negative number is subtracted from another quantity, the two negatives make a positive, so that the net result is addition. Therefore $2 - (-3) = 2 + 3 = 5$ and $3 - (-2) = 3 + 2 = 5$. We can thus divide both quantities by 5 to arrive at the simplified comparison below:

$$-2 + 3 = 1 \qquad\qquad\qquad\qquad -3 + 2 = -1$$

Therefore, **Quantity A is greater.**

17. **A and B:** For a product to be positive, either both numbers have to be positive, or both have to be negative. a and b are both negative on the number line shown, and so will yield a positive product. c equals zero, so anything multiplied by c will yield zero. Finally, d is the only positive number labeled on the number line, and so cannot be multiplied by another labeled number to yield a positive product.

18. **15:** Noting that $x^5 = x^{1+4} = x^1 \cdot x^4$ we can factor out x^4 from both terms, resulting in $x^4(2x - 30) = 0$. We can then divide through by x^4 because we are looking for a non-zero solution. This yields $2x - 30 = 0$ or $x = 15$.

19. **B:** Compare, Don't Calculate! When a power is raised to another power, the exponents are multiplied. Thus $(4^2)^3 = 4^6$ and $(4^3)^2 = 4^6$ We can subtract 4^6 from both sides so that the comparison boils down to:

$$-4^3 \qquad\qquad\qquad\qquad -4^2$$

Both sides are negative; however, because $4^3 > 4^2$, Quantity A is more negative. Therefore **Quantity B is greater.**

20. **B:** The prime factorization of a is $2 \times 2 \times 5 \times 7$ and the prime factorization of b is 3×11. Thus even though b is much smaller than a, the largest prime factor of b is larger than that of a. **Quantity B is therefore greater.**

Number Properties: Medium Practice Question Solutions

1. **B, E, and H**: The question stem indicates that the number line described must include 10 tick marks. Thus there must be exactly *nine* intervals (always one fewer intervals between tick marks than tick marks themselves—see diagram below, starting at some constant c and ending in $c + 9p$). Therefore, the correct answer must be *nine* times a prime number, since p is prime and there are nine intervals. Choice B = 2×9, Choice E = 3×9, and H = 13×9. 2, 3, and 13 are all prime numbers, so those answers are correct. All other answer choices are not multiples of 9, except for G, which is 4×9, and 4 is non-prime.

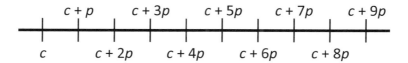

2. **D**: Since we know that $\dfrac{x}{100}$ is an integer, we know that x is divisible by 100. However, that *does not* mean that x must be a positive multiple of 100. It could also be 0, −100, −200, etc.

If x is a negative number, then x^3 will also be negative, but x^2 will be positive, making Quantity B greater. (The same would be true if $x = 0$.) However, if x is 100, then $x^3 = 1{,}000{,}000$, while $x^2 + 100 = 10{,}100$, making Quantity A greater. (Note that if x is any positive multiple of 100, Quantity A will always be greater.) Thus **the relationship cannot be determined** because the sign of x is unknown.

3. **B**: X originally contains the integers 0, 1, 2, 3, and 4. (Note that we do not include the endpoints −1 and 5, because x must be *strictly* larger than −1 and *strictly* less than 5.) Y originally contains the integers 6, 7, 8, 9, and 10.

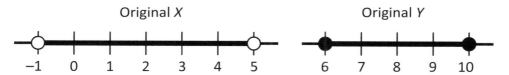

When X is shifted by 5 in the positive direction, it now contains the integers 5, 6, 7, 8, and 9. (Note again that we do include the endpoints 4 and 10.) When Y is shifted by 2 in the positive direction, it now contains the integers 8, 9, 10, 11, and 12.

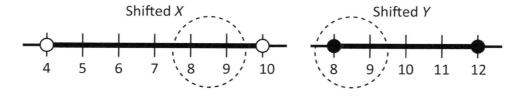

Only the integers 8 and 9 are found in both the new X and the new Y. The answer is 2, which is Choice B.

4. A: These values are too big to calculate using the calculator. Simplify the equation on the left as follows:

$$(7^{21} + 7^{-21})^2 =$$
$$(7^{21} + 7^{-21})(7^{21} + 7^{-21}) =$$
$$(7^{21})(7^{21}) + (7^{-21})(7^{21}) + (7^{21})(7^{-21}) + (7^{-21})(7^{-21}) =$$
$$(7^{42}) + (7^0) + (7^0) + (7^{-42}) =$$
$$(7^{42}) + 2 + (7^{-42})$$

The problem then simplifies to:

$$7^{42} + 7^{-42} + 2 \qquad\qquad\qquad 7^{42} + 7^{-42}$$

Therefore **Quantity A has a greater value.**

5. B and C: We can rewrite the original inequality as $|a + b| < c + d$. Since $|a + b|$ is non-negative by definition and $(c + d)$ has a greater value, $(c + d)$ must be positive, so Choice C is correct. Next we note that if $c < 0$, then the expression $|a + b| - c$ must be positive, since $|a + b|$ is non-negative and a non-negative number minus a negative number MUST be positive. Thus d is positive whenever c is negative. Therefore, Choice B is true.

Choice A can be eliminated because even if $a + b$ has a non-positive value, $|a + b|$ must be non-negative. Thus the sign of $a + b$ is unknown. To convince yourself, pick numbers, such as: $(a + b) = -5$, $c = 3$ and $d = 4$. The original inequality would hold. But the initial inequality would also hold if $(a + b) = 5$, $c = 3$ and $d = 4$.

6. A: To solve for the square root of any number which is not a perfect square, ultimately we need the prime factors of the number. However, because there is addition in the expression under the radical, we *cannot* split the expression into two separate radicals:

$\sqrt{81 + 169} = \sqrt{250} = \sqrt{10 \times 25} = \sqrt{2 \times 5 \times 5 \times 5}$. This expression can be rewritten as $\sqrt{2 \times 5} \times \sqrt{5 \times 5} = \sqrt{10} \times 5 = 5\sqrt{10}$.

Note again that we *cannot* split expressions under the radical. In other words, splitting $81+169$ into $\sqrt{81} + \sqrt{169}$ is *incorrect*, and will lead to the incorrect answer (in this case, Choice B).

An alternative would be to use the calculator's square root button!

7. B: First, we should determine the smallest and largest multiples of 11 that fall in the desired interval. The smallest is $10 \times 11 = 110$, while the largest is $90 \times 11 = 990$. Thus, the problem boils down to determining how many integers are in the sequence 110, 121, 132, ... 990, which is the same as the number of integers in the sequence 10, 11, ..., 90 (simply take the original sequence and divide *every* item in it by 11). This can be determined by subtracting the smallest from the largest, and adding 1: $90 - 10 + 1 = 81$. Note that it is incorrect to subtract 100 from 1,000 and then divide by 11, because neither 100 nor 1,000 are multiples of 11.

8. 14: Note that each third will always overlap a ninth. Therefore, the question can be rephrased as "how many dark gray tick marks are there?" Since the line segment does not include the endpoints ($5 < x < 10$), from 5 to 6, there are 3 dark gray tick marks. Similarly from 6 to 7 there are 3 dark gray tick marks, from 7 to 8 there are 3 dark gray tick marks, and from 8 to 9 there are 3 dark gray tick marks. So, from 5 through 9, there are $3 \times 4 = 12$ dark gray tick marks. There are two more between 9 and 10 because we do not include 10 in the range. Therefore, there are $(3 \times 4) + 2 = 14$ dark gray tick marks.

9. **C:** It is important to note that the equation $|b - a| = 2$ tells us *only that the distance between a and b on the number line is 2*. The only proper interpretation of the equation is that it tells us that one of the following statements must be true:

1. $b - a = 2$ if and only if $b - a > 0$, i.e., $b > a$ OR

2. $b - a = -2$ if and only if $b - a < 0$, i.e., $b < a$.

We can easily prove that Choice A need not be true. Suppose that $b = 1$ and $a = -1$. Then Choice A is false. Similarly, suppose that $b = -1$ and $a = 1$. Then, Choice B is false. The important thing to note is that an absolute value statement tells us nothing necessary about the signs of the variables in the absolute value expression.

Only Choice C must be true. If $a > 2$, then b must be positive because the distance between b and a on the number line is only 2. Thus b must be to the right of 0 on the number line.

10. **B:** When an integer is raised to an integer power, it falls into one of 4 possible cases:

     1.   A negative integer raised to an even power   →   Positive

     2.   A positive integer raised to an even power   →   Positive

     3.   A negative integer raised to an odd power   →   Negative

     4.   A positive integer raised to an odd power   →   Positive

Based the information provided, we can deduce that x must be negative and y must be odd (since x^y is negative). Also, since t is not a multiple of 2, it is odd, so r must be positive.

We can now evaluate the choices. Choice A is false: (Neg) × (Pos) = (Neg). Choice B must be true: (Neg) − (Pos) = (Neg). Choice C is false based on the 4 possible cases listed above. And Choice D is false: $(\text{Neg})^{\text{Odd}} = (\text{Neg})$.

11. **A:** We start by manipulating Quantity A, breaking it down into prime factors for comparison with Quantity B. First, $(3^3)^2$ becomes 3^6, because a power raised to another power is simplified by multiplying the exponents. $(15)^3$ can be written as $[(3)(5)]^3$, and the exponents can then be distributed, yielding $3^3 5^3$. The numerator in Quantity A can thus be written as $3^6 3^3 5^3$. Since exponents with the same base are combined with addition, $3^6 3^3$ becomes $3^{6+3} = 3^9$, and the numerator simplifies to $3^9 5^3$. Finally, since any number divided by itself yields 1, the 5^3 in the denominator cancels the 5^3 in the numerator and Quantity A reduces to 3^9. The comparison then becomes:

$$3^9 \hspace{5cm} 3^8$$

Thus **Quantity A is larger.**

12. **D:** If p and q are different prime numbers, then either could equal 2. Therefore Choices A, B and C could all be even. Similarly, a could be odd or even, as could q, so Choice E is incorrect.

If a and b are consecutive integers, one must be odd and the other even. Thus their sum will be odd. If in doubt, pick representative values (e.g., $a = 3$ and $b = 4$, or $a = 8$ and $b = 9$, etc.).

13. **A:** The quickest way to solve this question is to use the calculator. 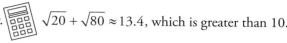 $\sqrt{20} + \sqrt{80} \approx 13.4$, which is greater than 10.

Alternatively, we could simplify the roots. A sum of two roots *cannot* be rewritten as a single square root, i.e., $\sqrt{20} + \sqrt{80} \neq \sqrt{20+80} \neq \sqrt{100} \neq 10$. Instead, we should simplify the two roots in Quantity A as much as possible, by factoring out a perfect square from inside the root. This yields $\sqrt{20} = \sqrt{4 \times 5} = \sqrt{4} \times \sqrt{5} = 2\sqrt{5}$ and $\sqrt{80} = \sqrt{16 \times 5} = \sqrt{16} \times \sqrt{5} = 4\sqrt{5}$. The proper comparison is therefore:

$$2\sqrt{5} + 4\sqrt{5} = 6\sqrt{5} \qquad\qquad\qquad\qquad 10$$

$\sqrt{5}$ is bigger than $\sqrt{4}$, so $\sqrt{5}$ is bigger than 2. Thus $6\sqrt{5}$ is bigger than 12. **Quantity A is greater**.

14. **D:** The only way *a* can be greater than *b*, while the absolute value of *b* is greater than the absolute value of *a*, is for *b* to be negative. Given that $a > b$, if both were positive, then the absolute value of *a* would have to be greater than the absolute value of *b*. Also, because *a* is greater than *b*, it is impossible for *a* to be negative while *b* is positive. But it is still possible for both *a* and *b* to be negative.

If both *a* and *b* are negative, then both quantities are negative. For instance, if $a = -2$ and $b = -3$ then $ab^2 = -18$ and $a^2b = -12$ such that Quantity B is greater. On the other hand, if *a* is positive, for example $a = 2$ and $b = -3$ then $ab^2 = 18$ and $a^2b = -12$, such that Quantity A is greater.

Therefore **we do not have enough information** to determine which quantity is greater.

15. **D:** For a sum to yield an even answer, either both terms must be even, or both terms must be odd. In contrast, a product will be even as long as *either* of the two terms is even. Thus q^2 and qr will be even, whereas r^2 will be odd.

Now, look at the sums: Choices A, B, C and E all consist of one even and one odd term, so the sum for each will be odd. Only in Choice D do we see the sum of two even terms, so Choice D is the correct answer.

Of course, problems involving odds and evens can also be solved effectively by picking numbers. For example, we might pick $q = 2$ and $r = 3$. (We used 3 instead of 1 for *r* because 1 sometimes leads to unusual results, and is thus usually not a good number to choose when using number picking strategies.) With those values, the five answer choices yield 5, 7, 11, 8 and 9, respectively, which confirms our assessment above.

16. **D:** When two even numbers are multiplied, the result is always divisible by 4. This is because each of the even factors contributes at least one prime factor of 2 to the product.

In essence, then, the product of two even numbers could be any multiple of 4, and subsequent division by 4 could yield any integer: 1, 2, 3, … Clearly the last digit of this quotient can be less than or greater than 5.

For a concrete example, consider first the case $m = 2 \cdot 4 = 8$. In that case, the last digit of $\dfrac{m}{4}$ is 2, which is less than 5.

On the other hand, when $m = 6 \cdot 4 = 24$, the last digit of $\dfrac{m}{4}$ is 6, which is greater than 5.

Therefore **we do not have enough information** to determine which quantity is greater.

17. **D:** A product is positive either if both terms are positive, or both terms are negative. Looking at Choice A, we see that the product uv is positive; however, that product is subtracted from another positive quantity, w. The result may or may not be positive. In Choice B, a negative quantity (vw) is subtracted from another negative quantity, u. The result is once again indeterminate: If wv is more negative than u, then the result of the subtraction operation would be positive, but otherwise it would be negative. The other three answer choices are all products. In Choice C, $w - v$, which is positive (because w is greater than v), is multiplied by the negative quantity, u. The result will be negative. Choice E is also the product of one positive and one negative quantity. By contrast, in Choice D, two negative terms are multiplied together, as $v < 0$ and $u < w$, so $u - w < 0$. Thus Choice D yields a result that will be positive.

18. **A:** One possible arrangement of X, Y, Z and W is shown below:

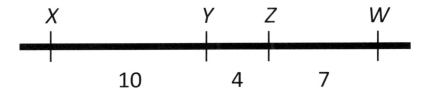

Here the distance from X to W is maximum (21). We can move W to the other side of Z for a different arrangement, such that the distance from X to W shrinks to 7:

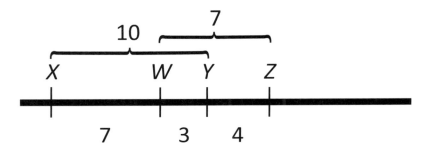

We can furthermore move Z to the other side of Y, so as to obtain a distance of 1 from X to W. This is the minimum.

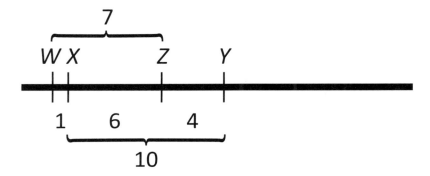

*Manhattan*GRE*Prep

the new standard

19. **D:** When a base to a certain power is raised to another power, the exponents are multiplied. When two bases raised to different exponents are multiplied, the exponents are added, and when one base raised to a certain power is divided by another, the exponents are subtracted. Finally, note that a itself has an implied exponent of 1. Therefore:

$$\frac{a\left(a^2\right)^{-1}}{a^{-1}} = \frac{a^1 \times a^{-2}}{a^{-1}} = a^{1+(-2)-(-1)} = a^{1-2+1} = a^0.$$

Note that this quantity will equal 1 for any value of $a \neq 0$.

20. **C:** Because the tick marks are evenly spaced, and because two of the tick marks are labeled with numbers, we can determine the distance between each of the tick marks using the formula: $\dfrac{\text{upper} - \text{lower}}{\text{\# of intervals}}$. Here, there are 5 intervals, the upper value is 0 and the lower value is −10:

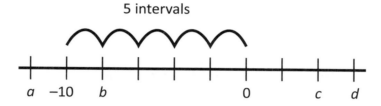

Thus each interval is $\dfrac{0-(-10)}{5} = \dfrac{10}{5} = 2$ units apart.

a is one interval to the left of −10, so $a = -10 - 2 = -12$. b is one interval to the right of −10, so $b = -10 + 2 = -8$. c is two intervals to the right of 0, so $c = 0 + 2(2) = 4$. d is one interval to the right of c, so $d = 4 + 2 = 6$.

The comparison thus becomes:

$$(-12)(4) = -48 \qquad\qquad\qquad\qquad (-8)(6) = -48$$

The two **quantities are therefore equal** and the correct answer is Choice C.

Number Properties: Hard Practice Question Solutions

1. **C and E:** The product in the question stem is the product of 3 consecutive integers. Any three consecutive integers will always contain a multiple of 3. Therefore, $(a - 1)(a)(a + 1)$ is always divisible by 3, so Choice C is correct. Because $(a - 1)(a)(a + 1)$ is divisible by 3 (among other things), it is non-prime, so Choice E is correct.

The other choices can fail as follows. If $a = 1$, then the product will equal zero, since $a - 1$ would equal zero. Therefore Choice A is incorrect. Since the product of 3 consecutive integers will always contain an even number, Choice B is incorrect—the product will always be *even*, not odd. Finally, if a is an even number that is not a multiple of 4 (such as $a = 6$), the product will have only one 2 in its prime factorization, so the product will not be divisible by 4. Therefore Choice D is incorrect.

2. **A:** The calculator is a bad way to go here. Use your exponent rules!

$$\frac{6^8 5^3 4^2}{3^6 8^2} = \frac{3^8 2^8 5^3 2^4}{3^6 2^6} = 2^6 3^2 5^3 \qquad\qquad \frac{6^9 5^3 4^3}{3^8 2^8} = \frac{3^9 2^9 5^3 2^6}{3^8 2^8} = 2^7 3^1 5^3$$

Quantity A has an extra 3 in its prime factorization whereas Quantity B only has an extra 2. Therefore **Quantity A is greater**.

3. **D and E:** These problems are most easily solved by breaking bases into their prime factors, and then grouping:

$$3^{2a} 11^b = 27^{4x} 33^{2x}$$
$$3^{2a} 11^b = (3^3)^{4x} 3^{2x} 11^{2x}$$
$$3^{2a} 11^b = 3^{14x} 11^{2x}$$

Because of the prime bases, the exponents must also be equal. This gives rise to the equations:

$14x = 2a$, so $x = \dfrac{a}{7}$.

Also, $2x = b$, so $x = \dfrac{b}{2}$.

All the other Choices may be true, for example if $a = b = x = 0$. However, only Choices D and E *must* be true.

4. **A, B, D, and E:** One way to solve this type of problem is to graphically depict all possible cases. Fortunately, the conditions given in the problem ($y > 0$ and $xz > 0$) limit the possible cases: y must be positive, and x and z must have the same sign (both positive or both negative), so we can answer the question effectively by picking numbers.

If x and z are positive, then either $y > x$ or $y < x$ (notice that z must be greater than y because they are both positive, and z is greater than $y + 2$). Consider the following two sets of values, which both satisfy all of the conditions: (1) $x = 1$, $y = 5$, $z = 9$ and (2) $y = 1$, $x = 2$, $z = 5$. These cases demonstrate that Choices A and B are both possible.

Choice D can also be true unless the variables have to be integers—which they do not in this question. Thus the choice is a trap for test-takers who assume that the variables must be integers. One possible example which would fit this description is: $y = 1$, $x = 2.7$, and $z = 4$.

If x and z are negative, then Choice E must be true—y is positive, and since $|z| > |x|$, it must be the case that $z < x$.

For the same reasons, Choice C cannot be true. If x and z are both negative, then x must be greater than z, again because $|z| > |x|$.

5. **51:** Since we are trying to find the maximum value of N (which we know nothing about other than that it's a positive two digit integer), and we know that N increases as M does, we should find the maximum value of M and solve for N. M cannot equal 99 since M is not divisible by 3; thus, the largest possible value of M is 97, which sets the maximum value of N at 51.

6. **26:** Every integer smaller than or equal to 11 is a factor of 11!. Therefore, we must evaluate numbers larger than 11.

12 is a factor of 11!, because 4 and 3 are both factors of 11!.

13 is not a factor of 11!, but it is a prime number.

14 is a factor, because 2 and 7 are both factors of 11!.

By similar logic, all integers between 15 and 25 are either prime numbers or can be broken down into factors that are factors of 11. 26 is non-prime—it has 2 and 13 in its prime factorization. Since 13 is not a factor of 11!, neither is 26. Therefore 26 is the correct answer.

(An alternative way of thinking about this problem is to consider the smallest prime number which is not a factor of 11!—13—and find the smallest multiple of 13 that is non-prime. This can be done simply by multiplying 13 by 2, the smallest prime number.)

7. **E:** The numerator of the fraction consists of three consecutive integers. Thus, the numerator will always be even and divisible by three (at least one term in the numerator will be even and exactly one will be divisible by 3). However, the numerator does not have to be divisible by 5. So, when $x = 0$, the denominator will equal 6 and the fraction will always be an integer.

8. **E:** If ab is divisible by c, then a might be divisible by c (for example, if $a = 8$, $b = 3$ and $c = 2$). Choice A is possible and thus incorrect. Additionally, this numeric example demonstrates that Choice C is possible and thus incorrect, since 2 is a prime number.

If ab is divisible by c, then a might also _not_ be divisible by c (for example, if $a = 3$, $b = 4$ and $c = 6$). Choice B is possible and thus incorrect.

In Choice D, if c is odd and $ab + c$ is odd, then ab must be even. An even divided by an odd can result in an integer—e.g., if $ab = 12$ and $c = 3$. Choice D is possible and thus incorrect.

Finally, in Choice E, if c is even and $ab + c$ is odd, then ab must be odd. An odd divided by an even will _never_ result in an integer—i.e., if ab is odd and c is even, ab will _never_ be divisible by c. Choice E is impossible and therefore is the _correct_ answer.

9. **256:** If $\dfrac{x^2}{4}$ is an integer greater than 50, then x^2 is an integer greater than 200. Furthermore, x^2 must be divisible by 4, so x must be divisible by 2 (even). Testing numbers, we can conclude that $x = 14$ is just barely too small ($x^2 = 196$), so $x = 16$ and $16^2 = 256$ is the smallest possible value for x^2. Use the calculator to test these numbers if you need to.

10. **E:** Simplifying will be easier than using the calculator here. We can either first multiply the parentheses (using the FOIL method) and then simplify, or first simplify $\sqrt{8}$ as $2\sqrt{2}$, group related terms, and then multiply. The first approach yields:

$$-(\sqrt{2} - \sqrt{8})(2\sqrt{2} + \sqrt{8}) = (\sqrt{8} - \sqrt{2})(2\sqrt{2} + \sqrt{8}) = 2\sqrt{16} + 8 - 2 \times 2 - \sqrt{16} = 8 + 8 - 4 - 4 = 8.$$

Alternatively, the second approach yields:

$$-(\sqrt{2} - \sqrt{8})(2\sqrt{2} + \sqrt{8}) = (\sqrt{8} - \sqrt{2})(2\sqrt{2} + \sqrt{8}) = (2\sqrt{2} - \sqrt{2})(2\sqrt{2} + 2\sqrt{2}) = \sqrt{2} \times 4\sqrt{2} = 4 \times 2 = 8.$$

11. **276:** Because the only even prime number is 2, m must be the product of $2 \times 2 = 4$ and two odd primes. Further, due to the restriction that m be less than 300, the product of those two odd primes must be less than $\dfrac{300}{4} = 75$. Thus

we need to find the largest number smaller than 75 that is the product of exactly two odd prime numbers. We can thus rule out even numbers. 73 is prime, as is 71; 69 is the product of two prime numbers (3 and 23). Thus, the maximum possible value for m is $2 \times 2 \times 3 \times 23 = 276$.

12. **B:** The product of x and y is negative, indicating that the two quantities have opposite signs. The easiest way to show that Quantity B is greater is to try actual numbers. For instance, if $x = -3$ and $y = 2$, then $|x + y| = |-1| = 1$ while $|x| + |y| = 3 + 2 = 5$. Intuitively, we can see that the sum of two positive absolute values will always be greater than the absolute value of the sum of two quantities, one of which is negative.

Therefore **Quantity B is greater.**

13. **B:** The number of zeros at the end of an integer indicates how many times that integer could be divided by 10. 10 has 2 and 5 as its prime factors. Thus, the number of pairs of (2×5) in the prime factorization of a number will determine the number of zeros at the end of the number. For the terms in the expression, only the powers of 5 itself can contribute 5s to the prime factorization, whereas prime factors of 2 may come from the 4s and the 6s, with each 4 contributing two 2s. Thus, $3^3 4^4 5^5 6^6$ will have $2 \times 4 + 6 = 14$ 2s and 5 5s in its prime factorization. The number of complete pairs of (2×5) is thus limited by the number of 5s; $3^3 4^4 5^5 6^6$ will have 5 such pairs, and therefore 5 zeros at the end. Meanwhile, $3^6 4^5 5^4 6^3$ will have $2 \times 5 + 3 = 13$ twos and 4 fives in its prime factorization. The number of complete pairs of (2×5), and thus the number of zeros at the end, will be 4.

Finally, observe that we will be subtracting a number that has 4 zeros at the end, from a larger number that has 5 zeros at the end. A quick calculation like $100,000 - 40,000 = 60,000$ should convince you that the result will have 4 zeros at the end.

14. **A:** In Quantity A, a negative integer is raised to a positive odd power. Odd powers retain the sign of the underlying quantity. Thus $(-3)^x = -3^x$. Meanwhile, in Quantity B, the exponent may be broken up as follows, so as to match that in Quantity A: $-2^{2x} = -(2^2)^x = -4^x$. Note that the minus sign in this case is applied after the multiplication, for both quantities. Thus, the comparison reduces to:

$$-3^x \qquad\qquad\qquad\qquad\qquad -4^x$$

Both columns are negative; however, for positive x, $3^x < 4^x$, so that $-3^x > -4^x$.

Therefore **Quantity A is larger.**

15. **C**: We can start by multiplying both sides by 3. This does not affect the comparison because we are multiplying both quantities by a positive quantity (i.e., the operation is "reversible"). Note that $3 \times 3^{18} = 3^1 \times 3^{18} = 3^{19}$. The quantities are now as follows:

$$3^{20} - 3^{19} \qquad\qquad\qquad\qquad 3^{19} + 3^{19}$$

We can now add 3^{19} to both sides, resulting in

$$3^{20} \qquad\qquad\qquad\qquad 3 \times 3^{19}$$

$3 \times 3^{19} = 3^1 \times 3^{19} = 3^{20}$, so the **two quantities are equal**.

16. **A, D, E, and F:** Any group of three consecutive integers _must_ include a multiple of 3. Therefore, the product of any three consecutive integers is divisible by 3. This shows that Choice A is correct, as is Choice E (which is a group of three consecutive integers, shifted upward by one from the original set). Now, if either y or z is a multiple of 3, then the expressions in Choices B and C will also be divisible by 3, but we do not know for certain which of x, y and z is the multiple of 3. Therefore Choices B and C should be excluded. Choice D, on the other hand, is another set of 3 consecutive integers and is therefore correct ($x + 3$ is one greater than z). Finally, Choice F is also correct, because $(x + 1)(y + 2)(z + 3)$ represents the product of three consecutive even integers or three consecutive odd integers (depending on whether x is even or odd). In either case, one of the three terms _must_ be a multiple of 3.

17. **48:** Because b, c, and d are all even, each variable has at least one 2 in its prime factorization, so bcd will have at least 3 2s in its prime factorization. Furthermore, because b, c and d are consecutive even integers, at least one of them will have an extra 2 in its prime factorization (because every other even number is divisible by 4, or 2^2). Therefore bcd will have at least one additional 2 in its prime factorization, for a minimum of 4 2s.

In addition, because b, c and d are 3 consecutive even integers, exactly one of them will be divisible by 3 (every third even number is a multiple of 6). Thus, bcd will have at least 1 3 in its prime factorization.

We cannot tell for certain whether bcd will have any other prime factors, so the correct answer is $2^4 \times 3 = 16 \times 3 = 48$.

Note that it is no coincidence that this is equal to the product of the three smallest positive even integers ($2 \times 4 \times 6 = 48$). The question stipulates that $2 < b$, and thus $b \geq 4$, to make number-picking less effective and thus make the problem seem more difficult.

18. **B and D:** Because x^2 is divisible by 40, which has a prime factorization of $2 \times 2 \times 2 \times 5$, x must have 2s and 5s in its prime factorization. Notice that there are <u>three</u> 2s in the prime factorization of 40, so it is not sufficient for x to have only one 2 in its prime factorization. If that were the case, x^2 would have exactly two 2s in its prime factorization. Therefore, x must have <u>at least</u> two 2s and one 5 in its prime factorization.

Furthermore, x^2 is divisible by 75, which has a prime factorization of $3 \times 5 \times 5$, so x must have a 3 and a 5 in its prime factorization. Notice that this 5 is redundant with the information we obtained from learning that x^2 is divisible by 40—the 5 in that prime factorization could be the same 5 in the prime factorization of 75.

Finally, the question states that x has exactly 3 distinct prime factors. We have already established that x must have two 2s, one 3, and one 5 in its prime factorization. Therefore, x <u>cannot have any prime factors other than 2, 3, and 5.</u>

Choice A has a prime factorization of $2 \times 3 \times 5$. This is incorrect because x must have a minimum of two 2s.

Choice B has a prime factorization of $2 \times 2 \times 3 \times 5$. This is a correct answer.

Choice C has a prime factorization of $2 \times 2 \times 5 \times 5$. This is incorrect because x must have a 3.

Choice D has a prime factorization of $2 \times 2 \times 2 \times 2 \times 3 \times 5$. This is a correct answer.

Choice E has a prime factorization of $2 \times 2 \times 3 \times 5 \times 7$. This is incorrect because x must have exactly 3 distinct prime factors, and having 7 as a prime factor would bring the distinct prime factor count of x to 4.

19. **106:** One way to solve this problem is simply to begin with the smallest possible integer for m (100 in this case), divide it by both 5 and 7 (checking to see whether the remainders are equal and non-zero), and continue working upward until a solution is found:

m	$\dfrac{m}{5}$	$\dfrac{m}{7}$
100	20 (Remainder = 0)	$14\dfrac{2}{7}$ (Remainder = 2)
101	$20\dfrac{1}{5}$ (Remainder = 1)	$14\dfrac{3}{7}$ (Remainder = 3)
102	$20\dfrac{2}{5}$ (Remainder = 2)	$14\dfrac{4}{7}$ (Remainder = 4)
103	$20\dfrac{3}{5}$ (Remainder = 3)	$14\dfrac{5}{7}$ (Remainder = 5)
104	$20\dfrac{4}{5}$ (Remainder = 4)	$14\dfrac{6}{7}$ (Remainder = 6)
105	21 (Remainder = 0)	15 (Remainder = 0)
106	$21\dfrac{1}{5}$ **(Remainder = 1)**	$15\dfrac{1}{7}$ **(Remainder = 1)**

This however is a computationally intensive and possibly error-prone approach. Instead we could rely on the remainder formula: $\dfrac{m}{y} = Q + \dfrac{R}{y}$, where y is the divisor, Q is the quotient, R is the remainder, and m, Q, R, and y are all integers.

(Note also that R must be ≥ 0 and R must be $< y$, because the remainder must be smaller than the divisor.)

The problem stipulates that $\dfrac{m}{5} = Q + \dfrac{R}{5}$ and $\dfrac{m}{7} = Q' + \dfrac{R}{7}$ (we use Q' because the quotients can and usually will be different) and that $R > 0$. Multiplying these equations through, we get $m = 5Q + R$ and $m = 7Q' + R$.

Therefore $5Q + R = 7Q' + R$, so $5Q = 7Q'$. This implies that Q must be a multiple of 7 and Q' must be a multiple of 5. If, for example, $m = 35$, then $R = 0$. If $m = 36$, then $R = 1$, etc. This holds all the way up to $m = 39$ ($R = 4$). If $m = 40$, the equation will no longer hold, because R cannot equal 5 (that would make it equal to the divisor in the first equation for m, which is not allowed—R must be less than the divisor).

This pattern will hold for all multiples of 35. The smallest multiple of 35 that is 3 digits in length is 105, and in order to make $R > 0$, we need to add 1: $m = 105 + 1 = 106$. This produces the result obtained in the table above, but much more efficiently, because we do not need to do any division at all, which is required in the number-testing strategy described at the beginning of this explanation.

20. **A:** The first step to finding the number of factors of an integer is to take its prime factorization. The prime factorization of x is $2 \times 2 \times 2 \times 3 \times 5$ and the prime factorization of y is $2 \times 3 \times 5 \times 5$. Next we can enumerate all the possible combinations of these prime factors, each of which must be a factor of the original number. Note that the combination which includes NONE of the prime factors is 1, which is a factor of all integers; similarly, the combination which includes ALL of the prime factors is a factor—it is the original number itself.

The easiest way to enumerate all the factors of a number is to build a factor pair list, starting with 1 and working upwards:

Factors of x					Factors of y			
	Small	Large				Small	Large	
1	1	120	$2 \times 2 \times 2 \times 3 \times 5$		1	1	120	$2 \times 3 \times 5 \times 5$
2	2	60	$2 \times 2 \times 3 \times 5$		2	2	60	$3 \times 5 \times 5$
3	3	40	$2 \times 2 \times 2 \times 5$		3	3	50	$2 \times 5 \times 5$
2×2	4	30	$2 \times 3 \times 5$		5	5	30	$2 \times 3 \times 5$
5	5	24	$2 \times 2 \times 2 \times 3$		2×3	6	25	5×5
2×3	6	20	$2 \times 2 \times 5$		2×5	10	15	3×5
$2 \times 2 \times 2$	8	15	3×5					
2×5	10	12	$2 \times 2 \times 3$					

Thus x is smaller than y but has 16 distinct factors, 4 more than y. **Quantity A is greater.**

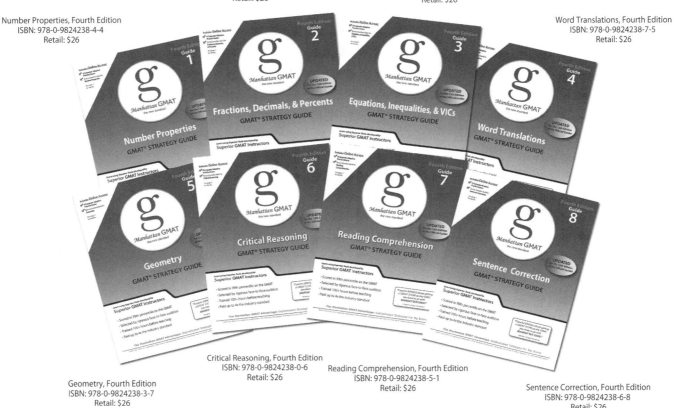